CLIMBING RULES & ETHICS

AN ESSENTIAL GUIDE FOR CLIMBERS

DAN GOODWIN

CLIMBING RULES & ETHICS

An Essential Guide for Climbers

DAN GOODWIN

ALL RIGHT RESERVED
COPYRIGHT © 2023 Dan Goodwin
www.dangoodwin.com

NO PART of this book may be reproduced, stored in a retrieval system, or transmitted in any form or by any means, electronic, mechanical, photocopying, recording, or otherwise, without the prior written permission of the author, except as provided by U.S.A. copyright law.

DISCLAIMER
CLIMBING is dangerous. Failure to follow the basic rules of safety can cause severe injury or death. Before taking any risk, please seek professional guidance and heed the warnings in this book.

COVER PHOTO
Dan Goodwin performing a Flag on Triangulation (5.12)
Location: Quoddy Head State Park, ME
Photographer: Anne-Marie Weber
All rights reserved

ORDERING Information: Exclusive discounts are available on quantity purchases by corporations and associations.

SPEAKING ENGAGEMENTS & WORKSHOPS are available upon request via
www.dangoodwin.com.

PRINTED in United States of America

DEDICATION

*I dedicate this book to the Climbing Community,
and to Keish, my adopted son,
who inspired me to resurrect this manuscript before his
spirit was taken away.*

*And to Cynthia Ado,
my darling wife, who encouraged me to "Finish it!"*

Author w/Cynthia Ado - Photo Joy Dutta

CONTENT

INTRODUCTION
Chapter One: <u>The Golden Rule</u>
Chapter Two: <u>Learn the Basics</u>
Chapter Three: <u>Learn the Commands</u>
Chapter Four: <u>Keep it Safe</u>
Chapter Five: <u>Keep it Clean</u>
Chapter Six: <u>Gear Up</u>

BELAYING RULES
Chapter Seven: <u>Pay Attention When Belaying</u>
Chapter Eight: <u>Don't Give Unsolicited Beta</u>
Chapter Nine: <u>Keep Track of the Slack</u>
Chapter Ten: <u>Refrain from Shorting</u>
Chapter Eleven: <u>Beware of the Fall Zones</u>
Chapter Twelve: <u>Know When to Spot</u>
Chapter Thirteen: <u>Learn How to Catch a Fall</u>
Chapter Fourteen: <u>Refrain from Lowering to Quickly</u>

LEAD CLIMBING RULES
Chapter Fifteen: <u>Inspect Your Gear</u>
Chapter Sixteen: <u>Wear a Helmet</u>
Chapter Seventeen: <u>Double Check Your Knots</u>
Chapter Eighteen: <u>Pick Your Routes Wisely</u>
Chapter Nineteen: <u>Learn How to Read Routes</u>
Chapter Twenty: <u>Know the Right of Way</u>
Chapter Twenty One: <u>Don't Hog Routes</u>
Chapter Twenty Two: <u>Clip Like a Pro</u>
Chapter Twenty Three: <u>Learn how to Fall</u>

TOP 3 LEAD CLIMBING MISTAKES
Chapter Twenty Four: <u>Back Clips</u>
Chapter Twenty Five: <u>Z- Clips</u>
Chapter Twenty Six: <u>Rope Burns</u>

MOST DANGEROUS
Chapter Twenty Seven: <u>Simul-Climbing</u>
Chapter Twenty Eight: <u>Simul-Rappelling</u>
Chapter Twenty Nine: <u>Don't Free Solo</u>

CLIMBING ETHICS
Chapter Thirty: <u>Don't be a Sandbagger</u>
Chapter Thirty One: <u>Protect Our Crags</u>
Chapter Thirty Two: <u>Support Our Rescue Teams</u>
Chapter Thirty Three: <u>Praise Our Route Setter</u>
Chapter Thirty Four:: <u>Be Social Media Conscious</u>

MINDFULNESS TIPS
Chapter Thirty Five: <u>Don't Judge</u>
Chapter Thirty Six: <u>Don't Compare</u>
Chapter Thirty Seven: <u>Stop Making Excuses</u>
Chapter Thirty Eight: <u>Stop Chasing the Grades</u>
Chapter Thirty Nine: <u>Trust the Process</u>
Chapter Forty: <u>Replace the Word "Take'</u>
Chapter Forty One: <u>Make Fear Your Ally</u>
Chapter Forty Two: <u>Be a Rock Warrior</u>
Chapter Forty Three: <u>Pay it Forward</u>

PRO CLIMBING TIPS

Chapter Forty Four: <u>Find a Mentor</u>
Chapter Forty Five: <u>Focus on Your Feet</u>
Chapter Forty Six: <u>Master Toe & Heel Hooking</u>
Chapter Forty Seven: <u>Become a Kneebar Master</u>
Chapter Forty Eight: <u>Master the Dead Point</u>
Chapter Forty Nine: <u>Focus on Your Breath</u>
Chapter Fifty: <u>Take Time to Train</u>
Chapter Fifty One: <u>Be More Flexible</u>
Chapter Fifty Two: <u>Take Your Recovery Time Seriously</u>

DISCIPLINES

Chapter Fifty Three: <u>Climbing Disciplines</u>

TICK TYPES

Chapter Fifty Four: <u>Tick Types</u>

CLIMBING GRADES

Chapter Fifty Five: <u>Bouldering Grades</u>
Chapter Fifty Six: <u>Lead Climbing Grades</u>

GLOSSARY

Chapter Fifty Seven: <u>Climbing Glossary</u>

ABOUT

Chapter Fifty Eight: <u>About the Author</u>

INTRODUCTION

"Some call it courage. I call it chalk."

Dan Goodwin

Before I begin, I want to share a story about the cover photo. I was born and raised in Cape Porpoise, Maine, on the street called Fisher's Lane. All my neighbors were fishermen.

My heroes were John F. Kennedy, Martin Luther King, John Lennon, Muhammad Ali, and Bruce Lee. I was the least likely person to rock climb or scale towering skyscrapers, but I enjoyed scampering up old-growth hardwood trees.

When I discovered Quoddy Head State Park, the most northeastern point in the United States, I was raking blueberries with the Micmac Indians in Cherryfield, Maine, crouched in a field under the scorching sun. It was grueling labor, but my revolutionary sweeping technique strengthened me. I stumbled upon Quoddy while searching the coast for sea cliffs on my days off.

If you want to see what it was like a hundred years ago, take the ferry across the Bay of Fundy to the Grand Manan Island on the Canadian side, and you will be in for a treat.

The Bay of Fundy is known for its extreme tides, with an average variation of 52 feet or 16 meters, making the bay the ideal location (upstream) for the Canadian government to install a 20-megawatt tidal power station. On low tides, you will see the locals digging for clams, wheeling their harvest in wooden wheelbarrows.

"Ready when you are," Anne-Marie Weber shouted across the cove with her Hasselblad camera.

Quoddy Head Light House - Author Collection

Throughout the night, I visualized the moves from the comfort of my van to the hypnotic sound of crashing waves and fog horns. I used the same mindfulness technique when I free-soloed Bagatelle 5.12d in Devil's Lake, Wisconsin. And when I performed a flag maneuver on Mickey's Beach Crack 5.12b for National TV and many of the world's tallest buildings, such as the World Trade Center. So, I was ready to take my climbing to another level.

"Climbing," I shouted.

If it's true, what we think about, we bring about, then what happened next was living proof. When I pulled the roof, I lunged up with my right, repositioned my left, then punched the flag for the count of three.

That's when I heard a loud...

KA-SPLASH!

At first, I thought I was imagining things, but when I lowered my feet and looked over my shoulder, I saw a giant humpback whale blast out of the water like a nuclear submarine and land on its back again.

KA-SPLASH!

Was the whale celebrating my feat?

I wanted to believe so.

Whales are one of the most fascinating creatures on the planet, known for their massive size and incredible intelligence. These majestic mammals have been studied by scientists for years, with many discoveries made about their unique abilities. One of the most intriguing aspects of whale intelligence, especially amongst Humpback whales, is their ability to read thoughts.

So, I took the whale breaching as a positive omen. When I reached the top, I changed outfits for the photo shoot, then free soloed **Yellow Dagger** 5.11 and **Stiletto** 5.12 - diagonally across from Triangulation. That experience was so magical; it gave me the confidence to capture the first ascent of **Maniac 5.13d**, the world's first route of that grade, a few days later.

Little did I know I would be authoring a book for the climbing community forty years later. A lot has changed since then. We didn't have the internet, cell phones, or social media. However, the rules and ethics are essentially the same, with a few exceptions: the introduction of climbing gyms and the Summer Olympics.

No longer is climbing a fringe sport; it's mainstream. With so many new participants, the climbing community must start talking about the things that matter.

In the 1970s and early 80s, we debated whether bolting on rappel and chalk was ethical. If you watch the video of my free solo ascent of Mickey's Beach Crack, you will hear me say...

"Some call it courage; I call it chalk."

That was my response to a fringe group that believed chalk was a form of cheating. We have come a long way since then, but there is a concern we could lose our way, which is why I felt compelled to make this contribution to the climbing community.

May this book serve as our guiding light and unite us as we strive to create the community we all wish to see.

Dan Goodwin on Maniac 5.13d - Photo by Anne-Marie Weber

Chapter 1
THE GOLDEN RULE

"Be cool."

Dan Goodwin

The Golden Rule is a philosophical principle that has been present in various cultures and religions throughout history. Its origins are believed to date back to ancient Egypt, where it was inscribed on the walls of temples as a moral principle. The golden rule simply states that you should treat others the way you would like to be treated. This rule embodies essential ethical and moral principles such as empathy, reciprocity, and compassion.

Empathy is the ability to understand and share the feelings of others. The golden rule requires us to put ourselves in other people's shoes and imagine how we would feel if they treated us in a certain way. Reciprocity means that if we expect others to treat us with kindness, respect, and fairness, we should also act in the same way towards them.

Compassion involves showing concern for other people's well-being and actively seeking ways to help them. The philosophy behind the golden rule is rooted in the idea of universal human dignity and respect for human rights. It recognizes that all individuals deserve equal treatment regardless of their race, gender, religion or social status.

The golden rule challenges us to go beyond our self-interests and consider how our actions impact other people's lives.

Therefore, make it your mission to be an ambassador for our sport. Not some territorial @-hole who thinks the crag or gym belongs to them. Strive to be a role model instead, not an example of how not to be.

When climbing outdoors, immerse yourself in the beauty of the environment. Refrain from playing loud music. Your music may help you get into the proper head space, but it may scare wildlife away and wreak havoc with the mind space of those around you. Wear headphones or ear pods instead or play nothing at all. If you can quiet your mind and listen to the fluttering leaves or trickling stream, you will be amazed at how calming it can be.

Remember, we are all members of the same tribe. Let us treat each other like brothers and sisters, showing nothing but mutual respect. Make it your daily practice to display random acts of kindness. Be the Appleseed of kind deeds and you will be amazed how it will impact every aspect of your life. Be cool my friends and good things will come to thee.

Chapter 2
LEARN THE BASICS

"Success is nothing more than a few simple disciplines practiced every day."

Jim Rohn

Safety is paramount in climbing, and understanding the necessary climbing techniques and equipment for a safe climb is critical. Learning the basics of climbing ensures that climbers are aware of the risks and hazards involved in this high-risk activity.

Safety must always be the top priority, and knowing how to use the equipment correctly, such as ropes, harnesses, carabiners, and helmets, can prevent accidents or severe injuries.

Furthermore, a clear understanding of basic techniques such as belaying, knot tying, rappelling, or abseiling ensures climbers can safely climb up or down steep rock faces or mountain peaks. A climber who does not know these essential techniques may put themselves at risk of severe injury or even death.

In addition to understanding these fundamental skills in climbing, it is also essential to be aware of weather conditions before embarking on a climbing adventure. Knowing when to call off a climb due to weather changes can mean the difference between life and death.

It's essential to start with the fundamentals, such as proper hand and foot placement, balance, and body positioning. These skills may seem basic, but they are critical for success in climbing. By learning the basics, climbers can confidently approach routes knowing that they have the necessary skills to tackle any challenge.

Moreover, this confidence extends beyond physical abilities; it helps climbers stay calm under pressure and think clearly in dangerous situations.

In conclusion, learning the basics is crucial for building confidence in your abilities as a climber. Respect for the sport is an essential aspect of climbing, and learning about the history and culture of climbing can give you a greater appreciation for this unique outdoor activity. Climbing has a rich history, with many pioneers who have paved the way for modern climbers. By learning about their struggles and achievements, you can better understand what it takes to be a successful climber.

Understanding the climbing culture is also essential because it helps you appreciate the community surrounding this sport. Climbing is more than just an individual activity; it's a social experience that brings people together from all walks of life. So, learn the basics, my friends, and prepare for experiences that will last you a lifetime.

Chapter 3
LEARN THE COMMANDS

"Communication is the key to every successful endeavor."
Dan Goodwin

Good communication is the key to every successful endeavor, whether it pertains to business, personal relationships, or a multi-pitch route in the howling wind. You may feel self-conscious shouting to your partner in the gym but remember, climbing may be an individual sport, but it is very much a team sport when it comes to lead climbing. Remember this.

After inspecting each other's gear, the belayer should inform their partner.

"You look good. Climb when ready."

When the climber is ready to go, they should respond by saying...

"CLIMBING."

Once the lead climber has made their first clip, the belayer should say...

"YOU ARE ON BELAY!"

However, the belayer should issue that command from the start if the first bolt has been stick clipped. Otherwise, the belayer is technically spotting until the lead climber has made the first clip. Some climbers like to let their belayer know when they are about to clip.

"CLIPPING"

If you fumble the clip, do not panic. Just take a deep breath, and let your partner know you will make another attempt.

"CLIPPING AGAIN."

This form of communication will minimize the chances of your belayer shorting you. We will get into shorting later, but the last thing you want when clipping is a taut rope.

You want the rope slack.

If you are unsure about the next move, give your belayer a heads-up.

"WATCH ME!"

When you find a resting spot, make sure you notify your belayer when you start climbing again.

"Climbing."

Otherwise, your belayer maybe caught off guard. If you need tension, and your highest clip is at your waist or higher, issue the following command.

"TAKE!"

This command tells the belayer to take in the slack and provide tension. However, if your last clip is at your feet or lower, you should shout the opposite.

"FALLING!"

Understanding which command to use can determine whether you will experience a soft catch or a hard...

KA-SLAM!

Avoid this mistake at all cost. Crashing into a climbing wall or a rock face can inflict serious injuries. When you reach the top of a route and clip the anchors, extend your arm and shout.

"YOU GOT ME?"

Your belayer should haul in the slack with the following response.

"GOT YOU."

Under no circumstances should you lean back and release your grip until you feel the rope go taut. Never assume someone has you.

Always confirm.

19

When I scaled the Nose of El Capitan in Yosemite Valley in 1978 with Eric Perlman, the producer, and director of the Masters of Stone series, I barely had a penny to my name.

I had to retrieve cans from the recyclable bins to raise money for a jar of Laura Scudder peanut butter, the only food we could eat because we were vegans.

It was late fall with a rumor of an approaching early winter storm, but we naively believed we could reach the summit before it hit.

That was our first mistake.

Our second mistake occurred at the pendulum swing. We were unsure what method was best for retrieving the haul bag, so we cut it loose, only to watch it bounce across the granite wall until it slammed into a ledge to the sound of shattering glass!

"There goes our jar of peanut butter," Erik exclaimed.

Despite our setback, we were determined to press on. However, two days later, we were on the final pitch as the sun set and the early winter storm kicked in. I would have given anything for a windbreaker and warm gloves, but I had neither.

You may never get tested in this manner, but sooner or later, life will deal you a deck of cards you never saw coming. Getting caught on the last pitch of El Capitan without proper gear was mine.

"Remember our signals," Perlman said.

I nodded.

We worked out our signals the night before at Camp Four, knowing there would be moments we could not see or hear each other.

"You are on belay," I assured.

20

For the next twenty minutes, I watched Perlman fire up the bolt line until the only thing visible was his flickering headlamp, reminding me of a snowplow vanishing into the night.

Then I felt a tug.

Perlman was communicating with me.

I felt two more.

That meant Perlman was off-belay.

As a rule, you should only disconnect from the anchors when your partner has you on belay. As soon as the rope went snug, I tugged back, indicating that it was me. Perlman responded with a triple tug.

I was on belay.

I quickly dismantled the anchors, then launched up the vertical peg board into outer space. I had no sense of up or down, like I was hovering in the cloud, but eventually, I joined Perlman.

As it turned out, descending to the Valley floor would be the crux of the route, but what got us to the summit and back down was our communication skills. So, establish your signals before climbing any route. By developing a clear and effective communication plan, you will significantly reduce the chances of an accident and increase your odds of success.

However, if you want to take communication to another level, consider a hands-free radio system. You will be glad you did on a windy day with the sun setting. You will quickly learn that communication is the key to reaching the summit successfully.

Whatever method you choose, if you prioritize safety and communication, you will enhance your life in ways you have not yet imagined and live to climb again.

Chapter 4
KEEP IT SAFE

"Accidents happen. Tragedies can be avoided."
Dan Goodwin

---

afety first is not just an OSHA slogan; it is about preventing injuries and saving lives. Accidents happen. Sooner or later, the unexpected will happen; when it does, you will be glad you read this chapter. As the old climbing proverb goes...

There are old climbers and bold climbers.
But there are no old bold climbers.

I could not agree more. I have lost a few friends that thought their luck would never end, but we all know that is not possible. Nobody's luck last forever.

When I met Dan Osman, a.k.a. Dano, the daredevil made famous for his unroped free solos and record-breaking rope jumps in the 'Masters of Stone' series in the mid-1980s, I was setting routes for a bouldering competition in South Lake Tahoe, California. Dano had no desire to compete, even though he could have easily won, he just wanted to help set routes.

It didn't take long to see that Dano was incredibly gifted as a climber. No matter how challenging I made the routes, Dano would flash them, forcing me to eliminate or change the angle of the holds until he could no longer send them as easily.

By the end of the evening, I learned a lot about Dano, as he with me. Dano had a difficult time understanding why I stopped free soloing when I was still in my prime.

"Why did you stop?" he asked.

"I didn't want to see my name in the obituaries," I joked. But I was serious. I knew if I continued that would be my fate.

"I would have kept going," Dano countered.

"Even if it meant dying?" I asked.

"Even then," Dano admitted. "I wouldn't want to die any other way."

Little did Dano realize, he had broken a cardinal rule about mindfulness. For what we think about, we bring about. Dano wasn't the first person to make such proclamation, and I'm sure he won't be the last. But every person that has uttered those words in my presence are no longer with us. So, be mindful of your words.

When I heard that Dano was attempting a world record for the longest rope jump off the Leaning Tower in Yosemite Valley, I figured if anyone could achieve such an amazing feat, it would be Dano.

But I had my concerns.

There are a few rules one should never break. Leaving your rope and gear exposed to the elements is a big one. Not only should you be concerned about the sun deteriorating the synthetic fibers in the rope and slings, but you should be mindful of the critters with sharp teeth.

Perhaps things would have gone different if the Yosemite authorities hadn't locked Dano up for two weeks because of unpaid traffic tickets. But on November 23, 1998, Dano took his last leap off the Leaning Tower, despite promising the judge to dismantle his rigging.

Miles Daisher, a famous base jumper, attempted to stop Dano because he was breaking all their safety protocols, but Dano went anyway.

Some believe Dano had a death wish and was setting a bad example. I want to believe Dano was attempting to do what no person had ever done before. He just lost count of his lucky stars.

You may think this has nothing to do with climbing, but keep in mind Dano was a world class climber. This fringe sport of leaping off cliffs with a rope began when climbers wanted to master their fear of falling.

Dano just took it too far.

We all know when we are being unsafe. Never pretend these dangers aren't there. Be the person that makes everyone aware and makes safety your number one priority.

If you heed this advice, not only will you be a shining example, but you will be twice as likely to be climbing at my age.

Chapter 5
KEEP IT CLEAN

"So many disease and illness have fundamental roots in the lack of clean water."

Jimmy Chin

Rock climbing can be an exhilarating and rewarding sport, but it's important to remember that we have a responsibility to keep the environment clean and healthy for future generations. As climbers, we have a responsibility to minimize our impact on the environment and leave no trace behind. Littering or leaving trash not only harms the ecosystem but can also ruin the experience for other climbers.

To maintain a clean climbing area, climbers should always pack out any trash they bring in and pick up any litter they come across. They should also avoid damaging vegetation or disturbing wildlife. Animals may ingest or become entangled in discarded items, causing them to suffer or even die.

To minimize your impact on the environment, always bring a small bag for trash collection. If you need to use the restroom or bushes, make sure to do so at least 200 feet away from any water source and pack out any toilet paper or hand wipes in a sealed plastic bag. If you come across litter left by others, do your part by picking it up and packing it out with your own trash.

When splaying your rope, make sure you use a tarp or rope bag to keep it clean. If your hands turn black while belaying, it's time to give your cord a bath with a rope-safe soap. When it's your turn to take a burn, give your hands a thorough cleaning with hand wipes, especially after going number two.

The same is true with climbing shoes. Refrain from walking in the dirt or into a restroom. This practice is unsanitary and it will contaminate the holds. Besides, you need to keep your shoes and hands clean if you want to be a sending machine.

When on a climbing gym, yoga studio, or fitness room, be mindful of your clothing and overall cleanliness. You may not notice it, but your body odor may make others want to leave the room. Do everyone a favor, take a shower, apply deodorant, and slip on a clean shirt. Your climbing partners will appreciate it more than you know.

By taking responsibility for keeping our climbing areas and yourself clean, we can ensure that our beloved sport continues to thrive while protecting the environment we enjoy for generations to come.

Chapter 6
GEAR UP

*"If you want to climb with other people,
you need to gear up."*

Dan Goodwin

Gearing up is not a rule, although it ought to be if safety is your number one priority. It is okay to purchase used equipment from a friend if you know the history and you can verify the condition by looking for signs of wear and tear, but be cautious otherwise. I prefer purchasing new gear because lives are on the line. I'm encouraging you to do the same.

If you can't afford the expenditure because you are in school or no longer employed, most climbers will be supportive by sharing. Just be mindful of how others might interpret your lack of gear. It is one thing if you are a beginner. Nobody expects anything from newbies. Most climbers are thrilled to see you taking an interest in our sport. But as time goes on, your partners will expect you to step it up, especially if you start taking whippers on their rope.

If you find yourself in this situation, the best way to express your gratitude is by showing up at the crag or gym with a brand new rope and saying...

"Who wants to take the first burn?"

If you embrace this attitude, not only will your friends appreciate the gesture, but it will supercharge your psyche because you have made the following declaration.

I'm all in.

Never skimp. Nothing will help you take climbing to a higher level than world class gear.

BELAYING RULES

Chapter 7
PAY ATTENTION WHEN BELAYING

"Complacency is the enemy of safety when it comes to belaying."

Dan Goodwin

Belaying is a crucial aspect of climbing. Beware of being lulled to sleep by a false sense of security. Complacency is the enemy of safety. If you are not vigilant, the consequences can be severe. Being tired or distracted can increase your risk of making mistakes or missing essential signals from your partner.

Secondly, avoid using your phone or engaging in other activities that could distract you from the task. It takes only a fraction of a second for a fall to occur, but in that time frame, anything can happen if you're not focused. You must always have your eyes fixed on your partner so that you can react if something goes wrong.

Several common mistakes can occur while belaying, which should be avoided at all costs. One mistake is failing to properly tie or secure the rope before beginning to belay. This can result in severe injury or even death if the climber falls. Another mistake is not tying a knot at the end of the lead rope. This can have devastating consequences should your cord not be long enough during the descent.

According to recent studies, 20% of all climbing accidents result from poor belay practices. In 2016, the free soloing legend, Alex Honnold, suffered a compression fracture of two vertebras due to a fall at Index, Washington. Honnold wrote this in the AAJ.

29

'I had run up the route Godzilla 5.9 to put up a top rope for my girlfriend and her family. At the last second, her parents asked us to hang their rope instead of ours. I didn't think about it, but their rope was 60 meters, and mine was 70 meters. I was climbing in approach shoes, and everyone was chatting at the base–super casual, very relaxed.

As I was lowering, we ran out of rope a few meters above the ground, and my belayer accidentally let the end of the rope run through her brake hand and belay device. I dropped a few meters onto gnarly rocks, landing on my butt and side and injuring my back.'

Alex acknowledged that several mistakes were made. One, they should have thought about the length of the exchanged ropes. Two, his belayer should have been paying attention (not talking). Three, he should have tied a knot at the rope's end.

And four, Honnold should have been wearing a helmet because if he landed on his head, he might have suffered a life-threatening injury.

Thankfully, Honnold made a complete recovery. The following year, he free-soloed El Cap, but his story only illustrates the subject of this chapter; accidents happen when you are NOT paying attention. It's challenging enough for a novice climber to trust their rope without worrying about their belayer; this should never be your partner's concern. They should have absolute confidence you will catch them. Most of us are guilty of conversing with friends as our partner ties in.

Still, once you have completed your safety check, you should end your discussion and provide your full and undivided attention. If you make it your mission to be the most attentive belayer, you will always have partners who want to climb with you. That is my wish for you.

Chapter 8
DON'T GIVE UNSOLICITED BETA

*"I just trust my instinct and move with the conviction
that I have made the right decision."*

Adam Ondra

Unsolicited beta in rock climbing refers to giving advice or suggestions to someone who has yet to ask for it. This assumption can be frustrating for many climbers, particularly those who are experienced and confident in their abilities. While it may seem helpful, unsolicited beta can be counterproductive, as it can distract the climber and lead to mistakes. There are many reasons why climbers may choose not to provide unsolicited beta.

For one, knowing what advice will be beneficial can be difficult without knowing the climber's abilities. Additionally, some climbers may feel that unsolicited beta is intrusive or even insulting. Ultimately, the best way to offer beta in rock climbing is to wait for the climber to ask for guidance. This practice allows the climber to take ownership of their learning process and develop their skills at their own pace.

While it may seem like you are being helpful and may have the best intentions, giving beta without being asked can hinder a climber's ability to learn and grow independently. When climbers constantly receive unsolicited beta, they may rely on others for guidance instead of learning to problem-solve and think critically.

I once knew a talented climber that fell into this category. Her partner would often send the routes with relative ease, but when it came to her turn, she needed to receive step-by-step instructions to send the route.

At first, I thought it was how they interacted with one another, but she tried doing the same with me when we climbed together.

"How do I make this move?" she pleaded.

I instantly realized this person was addicted to beta. So, I gave her some tough love. I encouraged her to figure it out on her own. Naturally, she was not happy about it.

No addict ever is.

However, she eventually figured it out and broke the spell. Today, she climbs a number grade harder and rarely asks for the beta. If you know someone suffering from the same addiction, try the tough love method and see if it works for them.

When I asked Adam Ondra, the first person to flash a 5.15 (see tick types and grades), what his secret was for on-sighting or flashing a route, this was his response.

"I just trust my instinct and move with the conviction that I have made the right decision."

And there, my friends is the secret to climbing without receiving beta. You need to trust your instincts. Never doubt whether you are doing the sequence correctly. Move with conviction and embrace this thinking.

I can grab those holds.

I can make those moves.

If you embrace this mindset, you will set yourself up to become a sending machine, and it all begins when you stop receiving beta.

Chapter 9
KEEP TRACK of the SLACK

As the belayer, you must constantly monitor the rope fed out to the lead climber. Too much slack could potentially place your partner in jeopardy should they slip while attempting to make a clip. Not enough slack will cause the lead climber to come up short. We'll talk about shorting in the next chapter, but avoiding either scenario is a balancing act that requires your full attention.

If you see the rope touching the gym floor or in the dirt when belaying outdoors, you have too much slack. I like to have a shallow dip (no more than knee level) in front of me. That way, I can respond quickly by either feeding out more rope or taking it in. Failing to monitor the slack can be a recipe for disaster. Don't let this happen to you.

If you don't feel comfortable, take a class with a professional instructor. When I first began belaying, I had major reservations because I knew the responsibilities that came with it. The thought of my partner getting seriously injured or killed because I failed to keep them from hitting the deck was more than I could bare. But it made me a better belayer and that is my wish for you.

Chapter 10
REFRAIN FROM SHORTING

Most lead climbers will agree, nothing is more annoying or frustrating than getting shorted while attempting to make a clip. Shorting is when the belayer fails to feed the lead climber enough rope to make the clip.

Not only is shorting an inconvenience, because the lead climber will have to waste valuable energy making a second attempt, but it can cause the climber to lose their balance and come off.

You will know when you are shorting when your belay device locks while attempting to feed the lead climber slack. If this happens, you will need to refine your technique until you have mastered the art of belaying a climber on lead.

If you are concerned about catching your partner should they come off, join the club. Every belayer should be concerned about catching their partner, which is why you should always be paying attention. But I get it, belaying can be intimidating, especially when your partner is on a route above their pay grade, and are struggling to clip.

However, if you are paying attention and providing slack when your partner needs it, standing in the ideal location underneath (topic of the next chapter), you will greatly reduce, if not eliminate 'shorts' altogether.

Chapter 11
BE AWARE of the FALL ZONES

The fall zone is one of the most crucial aspects to consider in climbing. A fall zone is an area below a climber where they could fall if they slip and lose their grip. Fall zones can vary depending on the discipline of climbing. For example, in bouldering, where climbers are only a few feet off the ground, the fall zone may only extend a few feet around them.

However, the fall zone can extend much further in traditional climbing or sport climbing, where climbers are higher up on the wall or on a rock face. Identifying fall zones allows the lead climber to take the necessary precautions, such as wearing a helmet or avoiding specific routes altogether. Another factor that can come into play is the terrain. If trees, ledges, or boulders are in the landing zone, the lead climber should proceed cautiously or choose a safer route.

Similar rules apply to the belayer. Avoid standing twenty feet back unless you are on a top rope. When you stand way back, you will not only create a ton of rope drag, but you will be twice as likely to short the lead climber. Don't be this person.

The best place to stand is to the left or right of the lead climber. Avoid standing directly underneath; this has danger written all over it because your partner could land on you. A diligent belayer will continuously adjust their position and stance based on their partner's location. One moment, they might be on the left; the next, they are on the right.

The only time you stand underneath, looking outward, is when the route is exceptionally overhung. This practice will be safer because the belayer will not be pulled into the wall and will minimize the rope drag so your partner can clip more easily.

Remember, you are an essential member of the team. Your partner can only climb with your participation, and their success depends on your rope management. Make it your goal to become a world-class belayer. Don't be afraid of it.

If your neck hurts from looking up (one of the reasons most climbers stand too far back), consider wearing belay glasses instead. These ingeniously designed mirrored glasses will enable you to observe your partner with surprising clarity and without looking up. I wouldn't belay without wearing a pair, and neither should you.

Chapter 12
KNOW WHEN TO SPOT

"Spotting is not a chore; it's a sacred trust."
John Sherman

The importance of spotting in climbing cannot be overstated. Spotting involves a person assisting the climber by keeping a watchful eye and potentially providing physical support to ensure their safety. This is particularly true when bouldering or lead climbing outdoors where the risk of injury can be great.

It is crucial to know when to spot in climbing, as it requires both experience and attention to detail. Spotters must have a solid understanding of the climber's abilities, as well as the potential risks associated with each climb. They must also be able to anticipate any potential falls and react quickly to prevent injury.

However, It's important to keep in mind that spotting can also be dangerous. If not performed correctly, the spotter risk catching a head butt to the face or a fractured wrist. So, never underestimate the force of gravity. Spotters should always stand in an optimal position (not directly underneath) where they can easily see the climber and have enough space to maneuver if necessary. Your job as a spotter is to guide your partner toward the center of the pad and away from danger.

Under no circumstances should you attempt to catch them unless that person is a child, and even then, be mindful. To minimize the risk of hitting the deck while attempting to make the first clip outdoors, I recommend using a Stick Clip, especially if the moves feel dicey. This game changing device provides top-rope protection for the opening moves and keeps everyone safe.

When bouldering or sport climbing indoors, there has been much debate whether spotting is needed. The climbing gym industry addressed this issue by increasing the thickness and densities of the landing areas to eliminate the need for spotters, thus making it the climber's responsibility to learn how to fall and land instead.

To everyone's surprise, the switch to higher-quality gymnastic pads proved so successful that the IFSC World Cup Bouldering circuit and the Olympics committee adopted this policy.

So, as a rule, unless your partner requests a spot, you are not obligated to do so when bouldering or lead climbing indoors. But if you sense your partner is in danger, you should do everything possible to keep your partner safe without endangering yourself.

When in doubt SPOT!

If you embrace these rules and add these skills and tools to your quiver, you will not only take your game to a higher level as a belayer and a spotter, but as a climber, sending harder than ever.

Chapter 13
LEARN HOW to CATCH a FALL

Lead climbing is an advanced form of rock climbing requiring different skills and techniques than top rope climbing. One crucial skill to master as a lead climber is catching a fall safely and effectively. You can use several strategies to improve your lead climbing skills and build your confidence on the wall.

First, make sure you have a solid understanding of the proper belaying technique. As the belayer, you must pay close attention to your partner and be prepared to quickly lock off the rope in the event of a fall. One of the most important aspects of lead climbing is knowing how to catch a fall.

Understanding the basics of lead climbing and falling is crucial for climbers who want to push their limits on the rock safely.

In lead climbing, the climber clips their rope into protection points as they ascend, rather than having a rope anchored from above like in top rope. As such, belayers must be attentive and ready to take in slack quickly to minimize the length of the fall.

When catching a fall, it's essential to maintain proper body positioning. The belayer should always keep their brake hand on the rope and be prepared to lock off if necessary.

To effectively catch lead climbing falls, belayers must also know how to use their belay device properly, understand how the device functions, and practice different techniques to arrest a fall, such as feeding out slack when necessary or locking off the rope quickly.

Overcoming fear and mental barriers associated with falling is crucial to learning how to catch a lead climbing fall. Fear is a natural response when your partner is about to take a fall; it can be paralyzing. However, it is essential to understand that falling is a normal part of climbing and should not keep you from progressing. To overcome your fear of catching a fall, start by practicing in a controlled environment like your local climbing gym.

But climbers be warned, catching a fall outdoors isn't anything like the indoors because of the dangers posed by nature.

In 2018, I climbed with some friends at Malibu Canyon in Southern California. We jumped on Mr. Big. 5.10d, a left-leaning bucket run over a large boulder underneath to warm up. I noted the danger but wasn't concerned because the route was relatively easy.

But when it came my friend's turn, I had severe reservations because he could hit the boulder underneath if he fell between the 3rd and 4th clip.

"You sure you want to do this?" I asked.

"Absolutely," my friend responded enthusiastically.

I could see concern in his eyes, but what was I to say? It wasn't like I could forbid him to climb, but looking back, I wished I had.

"Keep it together," I shouted. "You don't want to come off here."

My friend was staring at the 4th clip, paralyzed with fear after repeatedly dropping the rope attempting to clip.

"Then you got to down climb," I shouted.

My friend shook his head. "I can't."

"You got to," his wife pleaded.

40

Sensing danger, our entire squad gathered around the boulder to spot him.

"I'm going to go for it," my friend warned.

"No, don't," I shouted.

But my friend went for it anyway and came off while attempting to make the clip with the rope still clutched in his hands.

"FALLING!"

I leaped back and yarded in the slack as my friend flipped over backward and nearly clipped the boulder with his unprotected head.

I nearly puked.

My friend's brains could have drained out in front of me. Thankfully, my friend wasn't injured, but every time afterwards, where the lead climber is struggling to clip, I find myself dealing with PTSD.

You may think this will never happen to you, but if you climb long enough, it will be just a matter of time before it does.

So, master the art of catching falls, and don't be afraid to tell your friend to choose a different route.
I should have said...

"I don't think you should do this. Why don't you do a different route instead."

But I was more concerned with hurting my friend's feelings, which was my mistake. Had he been injured or killed, that would have been on me. Remember, as a belayer; this responsibility rests squarely on you. Never belay anyone if you don't feel comfortable doing it.

I got lucky.

Or should I say my friend got lucky? But I can guarantee I will never make that mistake again, and I pray you will say the same.

Chapter 14
REFRAIN from LOWERING too QUICKLY

You may think it's cool to drop your partner like a free-falling elevator, but when your buddy hits the deck and ends up in a wheelchair for the rest of their life, you will experience nothing but regret.

So, as a rule, always lower your partner in a controlled manner. You may think you're skilled enough to know the precise moment you should apply the brakes, but if your timing is off just a fraction of a second, your fun and games could end catastrophically.

And it's not just your friend's life you could be endangering. You could accidentally drop your partner onto an unexpected person standing beneath. Most people are not looking for climbers getting lowered, although they ought to be. The victim could be engaged in a conversation or getting ready to climb, not realizing their life is about to go through a transformational change in the worse possible way.

Do not be this person. Be the person that places safety first. If you believe climbing gyms have too many regulations, take your lack of responsibility elsewhere, but know you are playing with danger.

Sooner or later, gravity will win, and your partner will pay the ultimate price. But so will you in the form of guilt. So, refrain from lowering too quickly.

If you embrace this practice and make safety your number one priority, not only will you minimize the chances of such an accident from happening, but you will also live without this form of regret.

LEAD CLIMBING RULES

Chapter 15
INSPECT YOUR GEAR

I can't emphasize the importance of gear inspections enough. By nature, climbing gear experiences a lot of wear and tear. To keep safe, climbers must inspect their equipment regularly to ensure it is in good condition and will not fail when needed.

Failure to inspect climbing gear can lead to catastrophic accidents. A broken carabiner or worn rope can result in a fall that could be fatal. Even minor damage to a piece of equipment can compromise its safety, so climbers should take their time inspecting their gear. Common signs of wear include frayed ropes or harnesses or dinged carabiners. Ropes fray from rubbing against the rock or sun exposure. Worn carabiners can result from repeated use or drops from heights, while climbing harnesses wear out over time.

I last saw Todd Skinner after he captured the first free ascent of the Salathe Wall (VI 5.13b) on El Capitan with Paul Piana. The dynamic duo was riding high, but I had to say something when I saw Skinner's tattered harness.

"Dude. What's up with your harness?"

Skinner looked down at his harness and smiled like a proud father. His harness had served him on the Cirque of the Unclimbables in the Yukon Territory, the Trango Tower in Pakistan, and many of the most challenging routes in the Valley.

"Yeah, I know," Skinner admitted with a cowboy grin. "I've got a new one on the way."

Skinner knew he shouldn't be climbing with his harness, but he figured it lasted this long, it could last another couple of weeks. Don't make this mistake.

On October 23, 2006, Skinner and Jim Hewett were attempting to free-climb an aid route on the Leaning Tower in Yosemite Valley after logging more than a hundred days trying to piece it together. Then the unthinkable happened. Skinner fell 500' onto the talus field while rappelling from a ledge on the overhanging (110-degree) wall.

Not only did Todd's family lose a husband and a father, but the climbing community also lost a legend, a pioneer pushing the limits of free climbing on big walls before it became a thing. When the search and rescue team recovered Skinner's body, they noted he was wearing his harness, but the belay loop had snapped.

So, as a rule, always inspect your gear. Refrain from assuming your equipment and ropes are okay. Give your equipment a thorough check. If you drop a quickdraw onto the rocks, check if it got damaged. If you see a hairline crack, a dent, or the gate does not open properly, you should send it to the trash.

The same rule applies to ropes. If you and your friends have taken numerous falls, check for any soft spot in your rope. If so, you should cut the rope at the soft spot and use the remainder for something else. But whatever you do, refrain from attempting to squeak out the rest of the season with the same rope. That is a recipe for disaster.

Be the climber that makes safety your number one priority. If you heed this advice, you will reduce the odds of experiencing such a catastrophe and live to climb another day.

Chapter 16
WEAR a HELMET

The prevalence of head injuries in climbing accidents is a major reason climbers should always wear helmets. Statistics show that approximately 15% to 20% of all climbing accidents result in head injuries. These injuries can range from minor concussions to more serious traumatic brain injuries and can have devastating consequences. Climbers are at risk of head injuries from falling rocks or equipment and from falls themselves.

Helmets save lives.

Even a short fall can result in a severe head injury if the climber's head strikes a rock or other hard surface. In addition, wearing a helmet also sets an example for other climbers, particularly beginners who may not be aware of the risks involved in climbing. By wearing a helmet, experienced climbers demonstrate that safety is a top priority and encourage others to do the same.

A common misconception about helmets is the false belief that helmets are only necessary for those climbing on more dangerous routes or mountains.

Another common misconception is that helmets will limit a climber's vision or movement, making it harder for them to climb. This misconception is not the case, as modern helmets are designed with lightweight materials and offer a wide range of visibility.

There is also a belief that wearing a helmet will make a climber look inexperienced or weak, leading to peer embarrassment.

For example, in the mid-1980s, when snowboarding became the rage, I was among the first to wear a helmet at the Squaw Valley resort in Lake Tahoe, California. A few skiers taunted me until Sonny Bono and Michael Kennedy died because they weren't wearing one.

Within weeks, skiers and snowboarders began wearing helmets, and the climbing community is going through the same evolution.

While climbing in the American Canyon near Salt Lake City, Utah, my wife, Cynthia, was belaying her friend when she noticed what appeared to be a leaf fluttering to the ground.

At the last second, Cynthia stepped aside, and as she did, a rock thudded the earth where she had been standing. If Cynthia had not listened to her gut intuition, she might have been severely injured or killed, but that experience made her think about helmets.

She wasn't wearing one.

And that scared me because I wasn't wearing one either. As the most experienced climber, I should have been setting the example. I had a helmet in my pack, but I wasn't wearing it because I didn't believe there was any danger. Taking that as a warning, I vowed to wear a helmet from that moment forward.

You may think a helmet will make you look like a geek, but if you choose a color that coordinates with your attire, you can turn the helmet into a fashion statement, as my wife did. Nobody makes fun of Mama-C for wearing a helmet. However, there are no rules requiring helmets. That choice is yours, but you should reconsider if you want to make safety your number one priority.

In 2013, Beth Rodden, credited for the first ascent of Meltdown, a thinly protected 5.14c in Yosemite Valley, slipped while running it out on a 5.9 pitch of the Central Pillar of Frenzy. The next thing Rodden knew, she was falling backward, smacking the back of her head. Had Rodden been wearing a helmet, that impact might not have been an issue.

But that wasn't the case.

Later that evening, Rodden had difficulty concentrating and understanding conversations. That's when she knew something was wrong. The following day, Rodden learned she had suffered a concussion.

Concussions are a type of traumatic brain injury that can have both immediate and long-term effects. After sustaining a concussion, an individual may experience headaches, dizziness, confusion, and nausea. These symptoms typically resolve within days to weeks. If an individual does not allow adequate time for their brain to heal, they may experience long-term effects such as chronic headaches, memory problems, difficulty concentrating, or sleeping.

So, wear a helmet, my friends, and watch your friends do the same. Together, we will make our climbing community safer.

Chapter 17
DOUBLE CHECK YOUR KNOTS

Failing to tie into your harness properly can have catastrophic consequences, especially when climbing outdoors. Climbing gyms may have thick pads at the base but failing to follow through with your figure eight knot can prove fatal even then. That's why the belayer and climber should always inspect each before proceeding.

In 1989, Lynn Hill, the first person (male or female) to free climb the Nose of El Capitan in Yosemite Valley, California, intended to warm up on Buffet Froid (5.11) in Buoux, France. Lynn was engaged in a conversation with a fellow climber while tying into her harness and failed to loop the figure eight knot.

Nobody noticed this slip, not even her belayer. When Lynn reached the top of the route and leaned back to be lowered, she dropped more than 85 feet into a tree, where she crashed through the branches and slammed the ground. Everyone that witnessed the incident, thought Lynn had suffered a life-threatening injury, but Lynn only suffered a dislocated elbow and fractured bone in her foot.

You may believe this couldn't happen to you, but if it can happen to Lynn Hill, one of the most talented female climbers in the world, it can happen to anyone.

So, as a rule, always double-check your figure eight knot, and make sure you've doubled back your waist belt.

Never assume.

Verify.

This rule applies to the belayer as well. Always inspect each other before you say...

"Climb when ready."

If you make this rule a ritual, you will significantly reduce the likelihood of having an experience like Lynn Hill. That is my wish for you.

50

Figure-8 Knot

Chapter 18
CHOOSE YOUR ROUTES WISELY

"Our lives are a sum total of the choices we have made."
Wayne Dyer

Think twice before jumping on a route. Refrain from assuming a route will be easy and without risk. Train yourself to see the dangers lurking underneath. Is the risk worth the reward? Only you will know the answer, but listen to that whisper if it does not feel right. Your gut intuition is usually correct. I have retreated from more routes than I can recount (free soloing), all because it did not feel right.

However, there was this one time when I broke the rule. It was the spring of 1984. Money was tight. I had not done anything meaningful since my free solo ascent of Mickey's Beach Crack, and I was starting to feel like Charlie Sheen in the opening scene of Apocalypse Now.

I needed a mission.

And Short Subject 5.11d at Donner Summit in Truckee, California, was just what the doctors ordered. The route was a top rope. It was begging for a first ascent, but the bolting war was raging. Loyalists vowed to chop all rappel-placed bolts.

I just had my route (Apollo 5.12d) get chopped in Joshua Tree by the late John Bachar, and I did not want to deal with another.

So, I decided to free-solo Short Subject instead.

But as I stood at the base of this overhanging wall at 6:30 in the morning, I was severe reservations. I have never been a fan of crimping sharp edges over a talus field, especially at that hour. I prefer climbing later in the day when the temperatures are warmer.

52

"Ready when you are," my photographer shouted.
I nodded.
But all I could hear were internal alarms.
Do not do this, Dan.
This photoshoot could end badly.

I knew my voice of reason was right, but on this cold, early spring morning, I allowed my judgment to be clouded.

"On my count," I announced.

I removed my puffy jacket and gazed at the talus field beneath me.

"Three."

As the sun crested the horizon, I dipped my hands into my chalk bag. I had to look away as the early morning light leaked through the trees and momentarily blinded me.

"Two."

I gazed at the wall of painted granite and visualized the opening sequence. I instantly wished I spent more time on top rope.

Do not do this, Dan.

I tried blocking the voice, but it blared like a fire alarm.

"Climbing!" I shouted.

The exposure was instantaneous, like the bottom of the earth dropped out, providing a clear shot of the talus field beneath.

Do not do this, Dan.

But it was too late for that. My fingers felt like frozen sausages. I could not tell if I was over-crimping or not gripping hard enough. When I reached the heel hook and prepared for the dyno, my fingers felt like they belonged to someone else. Then it happened.

My heel hook popped!

For a brief second, I waged war with the force of gravity, desperately attempting to pull myself back in when...

My fingers popped!

I instantly knew I was about to face the consequences of all my good and bad decisions, but what happened next was short of a miracle.

At the last second, I contorted and landed in a manzanita bush protruding from an opening between two nasty-looking boulders...KA-SLAM!

I would not be here today if not for the manzanita bush and my forearms, which took the brunt of the force. I was so rattled; I was not sure if I would ever free solo again. Nevertheless, as my wounds healed, I had a change of heart. I knew there was only one cure for my malady.

A few weeks later, I free soloed Short Subject when it was more conducive for me (warmer) and without a photographer, capturing the first ascent without placing a single bolt.

So, before you get on a route, ensure you understand the risk and the reasons for doing it. Do not just jump on it. Be honest with yourself. Are you choosing this route because it is speaking to you? Or are you getting on the route to impress your friends? It is essential to keep your ego in check. You should reconsider if you are considering a route above your pay grade and the danger is high.

Remember, the decision to climb a route is yours and yours alone. Nobody can force you to climb it. If you do not want to climb it, do not climb it. Listen to your gut intuition and choose your routes wisely. If you heed this advice, you will live to climb another day.

Dan Goodwin on Short Subject Photo by Anne-Marie Weber

Chapter 19
LEARN HOW TO READ ROUTES

"Visualizing is the key to sending!"

Dan Goodwin

Understanding the basics of route reading is essential for any climber who wants to progress and climb harder routes. Route reading involves analyzing a climbing route before attempting it, and understanding the sequence of moves required to complete it.

The first step in route reading is to study the route from a distance, paying attention to its overall features and potential crux sections. Once you have an idea of the overall layout of the route, it's time to focus on individual moves. This involves breaking down each section into smaller sequences and identifying any potential challenges and resting opportunities.

Another important aspect of route reading is visualizing yourself completing the climb successfully. This mental rehearsal can help build confidence and prepare you for any challenges that may arise during the climb. By understanding the basics of route reading, climbers can improve their ability to analyze routes accurately and plan their moves accordingly. With practice, this skill can lead to improved climbing performance and a greater sense of satisfaction on challenging climbs.

So, as a rule, only jump on a route after giving it a thorough review. Analyze the opening sequence and determine the best stance to make your first clip, and all the potential rest spots. Then continue visualizing the moves until you have a battle plan.

Plans may change midway because the holds weren't as good as you thought, but having some form of a strategy is better than none. When examining the holds, try to determine whether you should grab the hold with your right or the left. Would it be better to cross and bump to the next hold or to go straight up?

You will not know until you get on the route, but if you can become an expert in visualizing the sequence, always looking multiple moves ahead as you would with a game of chess, you will dramatically improve your odds of sending the route on your first try.

Adam Ondra, arguably one of the best climbers on the planet, has taken the art of reading a route to a new level by becoming the first person to flash a 5.15/9a+. How is that possible?

Ondra mastered the art of visualizing the moves, and he trusted his instinct with the unwavering belief he could achieve such a feat. And there, my friends, is the secret as to how you can become a sending machine.

Chapter 20
KNOW THE RIGHT OF WAY

"Our lives are a sum total of the choices we have made."
Wayne Dyer

Who has the right of way has been the topic of many great debates, especially with the explosive growth of climbing gyms. According to the American Alpine Club, nearly 8 million Americans participate in our sport. No wonder climbing areas and gyms feel crowded, which always leads to this question.

Who has the right of way?

Is it the party that arrived at the route first? Or is it the group that roped up first? Most agree that it depends on the circumstances. If it is a multi-pitch route outdoors, having the fastest party go first makes sense to avoid bottlenecks and the need to climb over each other, but you will never know if you do not ask.

Always ask.

Never assume.

This rule also holds with single-pitch routes, whether climbing in a gym or outdoors. If you are in a rush and the other party is standing around talking, ask if they mind if you jump on first. Most likely, they will give you their blessing, but be honest if you intend to have a hangdog session.

They may provide a different answer, which brings us back to the Golden Rule.

Be cool.

We all know what's right. When top roping, be mindful of lead climbers. They may want to send the same route as you.

So, as a rule, know that lead climbers have the right of way if they are preparing to get on the wall before you. Do not assume you have the right to top-rope a route because a rope is dangling,

Always ask.

There is a chance the lead party may be climbing a route that will not interfere with yours, but you will never know unless you ask.

When outdoors, be mindful when setting up multiple top ropes. There may be others wishing to climb the same route on lead. If this happens, pull your rope after you have taken a burn, then watch and learn.

Do not be the person that keeps another climber from getting on a route. Not only will you be a better person, but you could also make a friend for life, and who knows, have the same courtesy shown to you someday. How cool would that be?

Chapter 21
DON'T HOG ROUTES

"What goes around comes around."

Unknown

As a rule, don't project a route if there are climbers waiting in the wings, especially if they are splaying their rope. Take this as a cue, for that route may have a small window of peak sending opportunities due to ideal temperatures, remaining daylight, or time.

This rule pertains to both indoors and outdoors. Don't be the person that prevents another from having their opportunity. Be the person that pulls the rope and cheers them on. You could be in for a show and make a lifelong friend in the process.

The same rule applies to your belayer. They may not say anything at first, but if you stay on the wall for thirty minutes, you may never get them to belay you again. True, time has a way of flying by when you are working a route, but that's probably not the case for your belayer. Twenty minutes can seem like an eternity.

So, as a rule, if you are getting shut down, and each effort is worse than the last, you might want to consider giving your belayer a break.

There is, however, a debate as to whether this rule applies to lap days. Is it considered good etiquette to occupy the wall for laps?

I think it depends on whether the gym or crag is packed. I'm a huge fan of doing laps. It's one of the fastest ways of increasing your endurance and fitness level, but I believe most would agree, if there are people waiting for a turn, not letting someone take a burn is inconsiderate.

Pick a different day or another hour of the day. As for setting up multiple top ropes at an outdoor crag, that's another topic of great debate. Is it considered good etiquette?

Again, I believe that depends on the circumstances. If its mid-week and nobody is at the crag, have at it, but if it's a crowded weekend and you are taking up routes that are often led, you might want to reconsider.

If you are a lead climber and you encounter this scenario, refrain from passing judgment for you initially learned how to climb on top rope as well. Not everyone can get into the right mind space when lead climbing outdoors. Leading outdoors can be intimidating, and it is dangerous.

It's not at all like climbing indoors.

So, it's important to keep things in perspective. Use this as an opportunity to set a good example by asking...

"Do you mind if I lead this route? I can set up your top rope afterwards?"

More than likely, they will say "Sure, have at it," and will be thrilled to watch someone lead it. But remember, if you find yourself in this situation, where you encounter a group of climbers top roping, don't take advantage of their kindness by turning it into a hangdog session. Nobody would appreciate that. You wouldn't either if the tables were turned.

It all goes back to the Golden Rule; be cool and considerate of others. If you are feeling guilty about hogging a route, listen to your conscience, it's usually right. Give someone else a burn and offer to belay. This attitude will go a long way.

Chapter 22
CLIP LIKE A PRO

"Knowing when to clip is the key to clipping."
Dan Goodwin

Choosing the proper clipping technique is crucial when climbing different types of routes. There are various methods for clipping quickdraws while climbing, and each has its benefits and drawbacks. Proper hand and body positioning while clipping can make all the difference in ensuring a safe and efficient climb.

Keeping your body close to the wall while clipping is essential. A proper clipping technique not only ensures the safety of the climber but also improves their performance. The process involves grabbing the rope with one hand, pulling it up towards the carabiner, and then snapping it into place with your other hand. To clip quickly and efficiently, climbers must practice their technique repeatedly until it becomes second nature. One helpful tip is to anticipate your clips. This practice will help you get into the proper position beforehand.

Overall, mastering the art of clipping takes time and effort but pays off in terms of safety and performance; clipping is one of the most essential skills to master. Proper clipping techniques can differentiate between a safe ascent and a dangerous fall.

However, even experienced climbers can make mistakes when it comes to clipping. The most common mistake is rushing when tired or under pressure; this can increase your risk of falling.

Another mistake is reaching to touch the quickdraw to see if you can clip it. Avoid this practice because you are only wasting energy. Trust your instincts. If you think you can clip it....

CLIP IT!

Yet another mistake is the need to clip the moment the quickdraw is within range. Refrain from this practice. Just because the quickdraw is within arm's reach does not mean you should clip it. Sometimes, climbing pass the clip to a better hold or stance is better. That sense can determine whether you will send the route or take a whip.

I get it.

Leading isn't easy. Often the most challenging part of the route is not the difficulty of the moves but the clipping. However, you can do a few things to make the process easier and more efficient without wasting a ton of energy. Clipping like a pro is one of them.

The first thing you will notice when you watch World Cup climbers is the speed and efficiency of their clips. They don't waste a second. Which method is best will depend on the position of the quickdraw and your preferred technique. Sometimes it makes sense to pinch the carabiner and flick it in with your thumb.

Others, it is easier to stabilize the carabiner with your index fingers before flicking the rope in, but here is your biggest tip.

The sweet spot for clipping is between knees and shoulders, where you can easily bend your elbow without yarding up the slack.

Think about it.

If you are continuously hauling up the rope to clip above your head, you will eventually nuke your shoulders.

However, if you are presented an opportunity to clip above your head, take it, especially if you can clip more than one.

This new skill will undoubtedly require hours of practice on much easier routes, but if you stick with it and make clipping like a pro your mission, it will just be a matter of time before it becomes second nature. But if you want to take climbing to a higher level, you must learn how to overcome your fear of falling, which is the topic of our next chapter.

Chapter 23
LEARN HOW TO FALL

"Master the art of falling and you will become the master of your fears."

Dan Goodwin

Learning how to fall in climbing is an essential skill that every climber should master. It may seem counterintuitive to focus on falling when the goal is to climb higher and stay on the wall, but falls are an inevitable part of climbing. By learning to fall safely, climbers can reduce their risk of injury by practicing proper falling techniques and using appropriate safety gear like helmets.

Overall, learning to fall safely is an essential aspect of climbing that can enhance safety and confidence. Despite all the precautionary measures taken, falls are inevitable and can happen anytime during a climb. Therefore, knowing how to fall correctly can prevent serious injuries.

One technique for falling is to keep your feet apart and knees bent like coiled springs. This technique will help distribute the impact throughout your body and reduce the chances of injury. Also, avoid grabbing a quick draw as you fall; this can cause severe rope burns. Instead, hold your figure-eight knot at your waist as you would on a rope swing.

However, it would be best if you practiced falling in a controlled environment like a climbing gym with the guidance of a coach or instructor. This learning method is the safest way to build confidence, so you won't be so intimidated when you lead climb outdoors.

65

In the 1970s and early 80s, climbing gyms didn't exist. If you wanted to practice taking or catching falls, you had to practice outdoors. My first opportunity was in Yosemite Valley with Ray Jardine and Erik Perlman, my climbing partner on the Nose of El Capitan.

Jardine wanted to test his prototypes for the world's first spring-loaded camming device called Friends. Many in the Valley were skeptical these devices could catch a fall, and an equal number debated whether Friends were ethical, believing they were another form of cheating.

I just wanted to climb.

So, when Jardine asked if I would be interested in testing his revolutionary new gear, I said...

"Hell ya!

Besides, I needed to overcome my fear of falling after climbing in the Gunks outside New Paltz, New York, with Rich Romano, the prolific first ascensionist, wearing only a two-inch swami.

Romano had one rule.

Don't Fall!!!

This mindset proved useful for free soloing and sending thinly protected routes with potential bone-breaking falls, but only up to a particular grade. I was always concerned about the consequences of taking a whipper on the swami belt. My fear proved so great I purchased a harness from the Rock and Snow climbing shop in New Paltz. And from that point on, I was no longer afraid to take a fall, but as I glanced down at Jardin's prototype protruding from the crack, I had considerable reservations.

"Are you ready?" Jardine yelled from below.

"Whenever you are," I replied.

"You can launch anytime," Jardine assured. "I've got you."

That's all I needed to hear.

I pushed off.

"Falling!"

The entire act of falling is usually over in under a second, depending on the length of the fall of course. As with standing at the edge of a bridge preparing to jump, the anticipation can be worse than the leap.

The same is true with climbing.

The key is to brace for impact with spring-loaded feet and your hands ready to protect your face if needed. Falling can be scary, but that fear will eventually be replaced with confidence if you continue to practice. That's what happened with me.

After taking more than a dozen falls with an equal number of inspections, Ray Jardine waved me off.

"I think we've proven they work."

I couldn't have agreed more. Not a single device failed. Granted, we were only testing three sizes, but Jardine's spring-loaded camming devices revolutionized trad climbing forever.

I never imagined taking 60-foot whippers for CBS Sports at the First International Sport Climbing championship nearly ten years later. I may have taken several hundred whippers before that event, but that experience would never have happened if I didn't agree to be a product tester for Ray Jardine.

So, as a rule, before leading outdoors, master the art of falling with the guidance of an instructor. Not all gyms offer such workshops, but if you want to pass your lead test, you must exhibit this skill set. But whatever you do, do not wait to take your first leader fall while taking a lead test. That is a recipe for failure.

Your first few falls may be terrifying for you and your belayer. Still, if you continue to practice mimicking various scenarios like falling while clipping, those fears will eventually become your greatest strengths.

Dan Goodwin taking a 60' whipper. Photo by Chris Noble

LEAD CLIMBING MISTAKES

Chapter 24
BACK CLIPS

Back clipping is the most common mistake made by lead climbers, and it is easy to make if you are not paying attention. The rope should always feed out from the wall, not towards it. If your rope points toward the wall, you have back-clipped. Don't panic, although if you fell trying to reach the next clip, there is a chance the rope will unclip.

So, as a rule, never take your eyes off the clip. The only time you look away is when you hear the click. You do not want to experience the horror of realizing, six bolts up, that you back-clipped the entire route. That realization could get into your head, preventing you from sending.

Hopefully, your belayer will catch your mistakes but do not count on it. Everything looks different from underneath. Besides, unless your partner is a veteran, the likelihood of them catching a back clip is slim to none.

Therefore, make it a habit to give your clips a quick check. Never assume. Always verify. If your rope is pointing towards the wall, re-clip. If your rope is pointing outward, keep firing away. Not only will this practice help avoid back-clips, but it will also keep you safe, so you can climb another day.

Back Clipped (rope points toward the wall)
Climber / Model ~ Apple Zou

71

Correct (rope points toward the climber)
Climber / Model ~ Apple Zou

Chapter 25
Z CLIPS

Z-clips happen when the climber accidentally clips the quickdraw underneath the intended draw. This mistake happens most frequently on sport and trad routes where the gear placements are exceedingly close.

Not only will this mistake cause instant rope drag, but it will also prevent the lead climber from progressing upward, and it could dramatically increase the length of the fall. It is crucial to note this mistake can happen to even the most experienced climber if they are are not paying attention.

The best way to avoid a Z clip is to pay attention to which quickdraw you are clipping and make sure that your rope is running straight and not crossing over itself between quickdraws.

When you become aware you have z-clipped, you should notify your belayer (always communicate) and correct by down climbing to the lower quickdraw and unclipping your rope.

If you are belaying, you should be on high alert while your partner attempts to correct this mistake, because even for the most seasoned climbers can slip while down climbing. If you see your partner making this mistake, bring it to their attention.

"You are Z-clipped!"

Not only will your partner be grateful for your astute observation, but so will the climbing community. Nobody wants to see anyone get hurt.

Z-Clipped
Climber / Model ~ Apple Zou

CORRECT
Climber / Model ~ Apple Zou

Chapter 26
ROPE BURNS

Rope burns suck. Anyone that has experienced one can testify to that. The burn can take weeks or months to heal and can happen in a blink of an eye if you are not paying attention to your rope. Understanding the causes of rope burns during lead climbing is the first step in avoiding them.

Rope burns occur when the friction between the rope and skin creates heat, resulting in a painful injury. The leading causes of rope burns are improper belaying technique (not wearing gloves) and incorrect positioning of the legs when climbing.

So, as a rule, remember your relationship with the rope. Otherwise, you could snag your foot and get a nasty rope burn. I learned the hard way at the Gunks outside New Paltz, New York when I came off with my heel hooked on a large overhang.

The fall was violent.

I could have easily cracked my head on a ledge, but I could not say the same about the back of my leg. I had a nasty 3rd-degree rope burn that took weeks to heal. However, I am happy to report that I have avoided making that mistake again.

So, never have the rope behind your legs. This practice is a recipe for a leg burn should you fall, and never grab your quick draw as you fall.

I made this mistake in 1983 while working on the first ascent of Maniac (5.13d) in Quoddy Head State Park in northeastern Maine. The protection was dicey; a few wire stoppers in the lower section and a handful of bolts leading to the top.

I trusted my bolts but not my belayers, who I recruited while raking blueberries with the Micmac Indians. It was just before dusk. I was gunning for the first ascent when I realized I could not make the last clip.

"Watch me," I screamed.

Fearing the fall and my belayer's ability to catch me, I latched onto the draw as my foot slipped.

"Falling!"

It was over in a blink of an eye. One moment, the webbing was firmly in my grasp, and the next, gravity ripped it out of my hand, sending me swinging towards the corner with a 3-degree rope burn on my hand. You may think this will never happen to you, but I hope you will remember this chapter when you are five feet above your last clip, unable to make the next. As a lead climber, you must continuously assess risk.

So, as a rule, if you cannot clip, notify your belayer "Falling!" and take the fall. The same rule applies to bolt hangers. Never hook your finger in a hanger unless you are willing to suffer an injury that could set you back for years.

Following these rules will reduce your odds of getting a nasty rope burn and make you a much better climber.

MOST DANGEROUS

Chapter 27
SIMUL-CLIMBING

"Always have three pieces in between."

Hans Florine

Simul-climbing is a technique used in mountaineering and rock climbing where two climbers move simultaneously up a route, with both climbers attached to the same rope. This technique is often used to save time and increase efficiency, but it can also be extremely dangerous if not done correctly.

During simul-climbing, the lead climber places protective devices while the second climber follows and cleans the gear. Both climbers move at the same time, making progress up the route faster than they would if climbing separately. The number of pieces and the distance in between will depend on the team's abilities and the risk they are willing to take.

Hans Florine, the author of On the Nose, who speed climbed the 32-pitch route more than a hundred times, and once held the record with Alex Honnold in 2012 (Time: 2:23:46), has made it a policy when simul-climbing to always have three pieces of protective gear in between. Florine's advice was for world-class speed climbers, not novice climbers learning how to lead.

Therefore, unless you are a professional speed climber (assuming all risk and responsibilities), the only time you should simul-climb is when you are topping out on easy terrain with a minimum of three pieces of protective gear in between.

Otherwise, refrain from simul-climbing. Take the extra time to belay each other safely to the summit. If you think lead climbing is dangerous, simul-climbing takes the element of danger to another level, especially when you start pushing your limits with less than three pieces in between.

It does not take a genius to see where it could lead. Even the best basketball players cannot sink 100 free throws in a row.

The NBA record is 97.

When simul-climbing, you are standing at the free-throw line. Sooner or later, you will miss or slip. Don't deceive yourself into believing you can do better. If safety is your #1 priority, you should refrain from this game of Russian Roulette because every time you simul-climb, you are squeezing the trigger.

This rule, however, is NOT to degrade speed climbing. I have been an advocate for speed climbing since I designed and constructed the dual speed climbing walls at the First International Sport Climbing championship at Snowbird, Utah. (1988). And when I free soloed both sides of the CN Tower in Toronto, Canada, for the Guinness Book of World Records, sending the first side in 58 minutes and the second in 1 hour and two minutes.

I'm simply trying to warn novice lead climbers about the dangers associated with this practice. As you will read in this next story, not even the world's best big wall speed climbers could escape their fate.

It was June 2, 2018.

Jason Wells, Tim Klein, and Kevin Prince intended to scale the Salathe' Wall on El Cap in a day. Wells and Prince intended to free climb the route, while Klein would play a supportive role by belaying and setting up a fixed rope for Prince behind him.

The trio scaled the 3,200' wall a few years back, so the team was familiar with the terrain, especially Wells and Klein, who scaled Salathe' 40 times, including a sub-eight-hour ascent.

Only a few climbers can make that claim.

The prior week, Klein had been named Teacher of the Year for inspiring confidence in his low-income students at Palmdale, California, an honor bestowed on him two years in a row. As a father of two boys with a loving wife, Klein had nothing to gain by taking unnecessary risks. Nobody knows what transpired, but according to witnesses and a follow-up investigation, this is what they believed occurred.

By early morning, the trio passed Jordon Cannon (a witness) and his team at Triangle Ledge before ascending the Half Dollar chimney, which leads to 250' of relatively easy (5.7) climbing to the Mammoth Terraces. Prince could not see his partners, but he heard Klein shout, "Your rope is fixed!"

Upon hearing those words, Prince began climbing. The thing about accidents is this; they usually happen when you least expect it and when you are thinking of something else.

Was Wells preoccupied with other thoughts?That's certainly a possibility. Wells could easily climb these pitches; he held the speed record on The Naked Edge in Eldorado Canyon, Colorado, so you have to wonder.

If Wells was combining pitches nine and ten into a single pitch, thus evading the necessity to construct an anchor on pitch nine, he might have been concerned his rope wasn't long enough.

So, there's that possibility as well, but when the investigators conducted their inspection, they determined the rope would have been long enough.

But Well's didn't know that.

It would be one thing if Wells and Klein had three pieces in between, but according to the investigators, they found no evidence of anything in between.

We will never know what caused the slip, but according to Jordon Cannon, who was starting another route that shared the lower pitches of Freebase when he heard a scream, then the sound of something falling.

At first, Cannon thought it was a haul bag.

Then Wells flew by.

Before Cannon could comprehend what was happening, he heard another scream.

Then Klein flew into view.

For a horrifying second, Canon watched the climbers bounce down the granite slab until their rope snagged a large flake, momentarily halting their fall - before exploding into a thousand shreds, sending both climbers 1,000 feet to their deaths.

Could this tragedy have been prevented?

Absolutely.

Had Wells and Klein followed Florine's three-piece rule, they may still be alive, inspiring others to pursue their dream, which is why you should refrain from simul-climbing - even on easy terrain.

You may have gotten away with it on occasion, naïvely believing this rule does not apply to you, but don't be deceived by that false sense of security. Nobody is immune. However, we can learn from our colleague's mistakes and take heed not to do the same. There are no guarantees, but if you make safety your number one priority and take every precaution, there is a good chance you will live to climb another day.

Chapter 28
SIMUL-RAPPELLING

"My greatest regret was not saying anything."
Aidan Jacobson

---

imul-rappelling is a technique where two climbers simultaneously rappel down a route using a single rope. This method can save time and can be efficient when used correctly, but it also carries significant risks. During simul-rappelling, the weight of both climbers is concentrated on a single anchor point. This can put immense stress on the anchor and increase the risk of failure. Novice climbers should avoid this technique altogether. Overall, while simul-rappelling may seem like an efficient way to descend a route quickly, it should not be taken lightly due to its high level of risk.

When the late Brad Gobright, 31, an American free soloist, teamed up with Aidan Jacobson, 26, to scale El Sendero Luminoso 5.12d, a 15-pitch sport route in El Potrero Chico, Mexico, Gobright didn't realize this would be his final ascent.

El Sendero Luminoso became a household name in the climbing community when Alex Honnold free-soloed the 2,500' limestone face in 2014. Many wondered if Brad was considering the same. We will never know, but if there was anyone that could have repeated Honnold's mind-blowing feat, it was Brad Gobright.

Gobright on-sighted all 15-pitches without so much as a slip. In fact, according to Jacobson, Gobright combined the first two pitches into one, making that single combined pitch a 5.13. So, there is little doubt Gobright was capable.

As to why Gobright felt the need to simul-rappel is anyone's guess. Some speculated that Brad was training for a mega multi-route day, a feat Brad achieved in 2016 when he scaled three routes on El Capitan (Zodiac, The Nose, and Lurking Fear) in 24 hours with Scott Bennett.

So, combining routes might have been the motive. But so was speed. In 2017, Gobright established a speed record (2 hours, 19 minutes) on the Nose with Jim Reynolds. When I interviewed Gobright for the <u>World's Most Dangerous Race</u>, he admitted that it was a number's game, but like many athletes, he didn't want to believe it was his time.

If you think simul-climbing is dangerous, simul-rappelling on big walls takes the risk to an another level. Instead of a single person rappelling on a doubled rope, two climbers rappel on the same rope, using a single cord like a counterbalance weight. Theoretically, if both climbers are equal in weight, lowering at the same rate, they should touch down simultaneously.

However, when Gobright and Jacobson arrived at the anchors on pitch 9, encountering two climbers from Costa Rica, they decided to rappel to pitch six with their eighty-meter rope. That decision proved to be Gobright's undoing.

Instead of unfurling their rope from the center to assure both ends were equal in length, Gobright tossed the rope over the side to save a few minutes.

Jacobson's end landed on a ledge.

Gobright's landed in a bush.

"I'll untangle it on the way down," Gobright assured.

Had Gobright knotted his end or tied the end into himself (recommended in high winds), they would have spent their night sharing stories and drinking Mexican beer.

But when Gobright rappelled down and attempted to untangled his line, Jacobson heard a POP!

That sound was Gobright's rope coming free from his rappelling device. It happened so fast; Jacobson didn't have a chance to react. One moment, he was watching Gobright untangle his rope, and the next, he was free falling, crashing through the shrubbery, and slamming a ledge. Miraculously, Jacobson only suffered an injured ankle. But Brad Gobright was dead.

When I spoke to Jacobson, I could tell he was still dealing with the aftermath - both physically and psychologically.

"My greatest regret," Jacobson shared. "Was not saying anything."

Jacobson had noticed that Gobright was not tying a knot at the end of his rope, something he had been doing from the top, but he was afraid to say anything because in his eyes, Gobright was one of the greatest climbers that ever lived.

Nobody wants to live with regrets, so let this tragic experience be a lesson for all of us. If you see your partner doing something that could endanger their lives, and yours, do not be afraid to voice your concern.

Say something!

So, as a rule, avoid simul-rappelling like the plague. Rappelling is dangerous enough as it is. In fact, more climbers die during the descent than at any other time. Don't be one of them. Take the time to rappel down safely. Double-check your equipment before making the descent.

Is the rope centered with equal lengths?

Do you have a knot at the end?

Is your rappel anchor bombproof?

If you make this a habit like a commercial airline pilot before takeoff, not only will you increase your odds of making it down safely; you will live to climb and rappel another day.

Chapter 29
DON'T FREE SOLO

"Everybody who has made free soloing a big part of their life is dead now."

Tommy Caldwell

The title may sound like I'm calling the kettle black (considering my history), but someone needs to be honest about the dangers of this forbidden art. If you thought simul-climbing was dangerous, free soloing is the equivalent of base jumping with a wing suit in windy conditions. At least with simul-climbing, you can minimize the risk by abiding by the Hans Florine three-piece rule, but with free soloing, the slightest slip could mean severe injury or death.

In the late 1970s and early '80s, I had the pleasure of bouldering and training with the late John Bachar in Joshua Tree National Park, California. Late at night, we would debate the ethics of climbing. Although we differed in opinion regarding rap placed bolts, we shared the belief that free soloing was the purest form of climbing.

However, I knew that free soloing was a number game. While Bachar seemed to believe he could continue indefinitely like a grandmaster who only grew better with age. Born and raised in Los Angeles, California, Bachar began climbing at a local bouldering area known as Stoney Point.

Within a few years, Bachar became obsessed with the sport and dropped out of college to pursue climbing. The lightning bolt on the Midnight Lightning boulder at Camp Four was first etched by Bachar. The Bachar Ladder was John's as well. But what really set Bachar apart was his free solos in Yosemite Valley and Joshua Tree.

Those feats made Bachar legendary. And that may have played into his demise at the end. The last time I saw Bachar was in Mammoth on New Year's Eve in 2004. I could tell John was still clinging to the past as if he could somehow make it last. I understood John's torment. It is not easy for a world-class athlete to no longer feel relevant when everything they did before made headline news. Free soloing was Bachar's identity.

As it was once mine.

But I knew if I wanted to climb El Cap on my 100th birthday, I had to refrain from free soloing, but I could tell John wasn't there yet. Five years later (July 5th, 2009), Bachar fell to his death while free soloing Dike Wall near his Mammoth home.

He was 52.

Nobody knows what happened, but one thing is certain, the cause of death was free soloing. Had John been lead climbing with his friends, he may still be with us. So, as a rule, do NOT free solo.

Don't deceive yourself into believing that free soloing will make your life better. Focus on on-sighting or flashing a route instead. You will get the same adrenalin rush, but without the risk. Or pick a project and train, but whatever you do, do not free solo. Not everyone is meant to be the world's greatest free soloist like Alex Honnold, and for good reason. Someone like Honnold comes around every 76 years like the Halley's comet.

So, keep your ambitions real and make safety your number one priority.

You will be glad you did.

CLIMBING ETHICS

Chapter 30
DON'T BE A SANDBAGGER

"Sandbagging is not only uncool, it's dangerous."
Dan Goodwin

Sandbagging in climbing is a term used to describe a situation where a climber or a route setter deliberately downplays the difficulty of a climb to make it seem easier than it actually is. This can be done for various reasons, such as to impress others or to gain an advantage in competitions.

Sandbagging can be dangerous, as it can lead less experienced climbers into attempting climbs that are beyond their skill level, putting them at risk of injury or worse. You may think it's funny to sandbag your buddy or a group of climbers from out of town, but your joke could cause someone to get hurt because they got on a route above their abilities.

So, refrain from being a sandbagger.

Sandbagging is not only unethical but also undermines the spirit of climbing as a sport that values honesty and respect for the challenges presented by nature. It is important for climbers to be honest about the difficulty level of climbs they attempt and encourage others to do the same. This not only ensures safety but also helps maintain fairness and integrity within the climbing community.

If someone sandbags a route, they are essentially telling others that it's easier than it actually is. This can be especially dangerous for less experienced climbers who may not have the skills or equipment necessary to complete the climb safely.

Additionally, if someone is sandbagged on a climb, they may feel discouraged or embarrassed when they're unable to complete it. This can harm their confidence and make them less likely to try new climbs in the future.

Sandbagging can also create an unfair advantage for those who know the true difficulty of the route, leading to a culture of elitism and exclusion within the climbing community.

It's okay to provide stiff grades in a gym to make the routes comparable to outdoors. I actually prefer it that way, but when route setters or first ascensionist intentionally downgrade the route so others will fail, that kind of behavior violates our code of ethics. Climbers should never do that to each other. Some may climb harder than others, but that should never grant that person permission to be a sandbagger.

Nobody has that right.

If you establish a first ascent, ensure the route is safe for everyone. Don't intentionally make the descent dangerous because you are trying to discourage climbers from visiting your area. That kind of behavior falls under the category of being a territorial A-h@le, and nobody like those people.

So, think twice before you sandbag someone. Be the person that provides truthful information and establishes first ascents where all your peers are saying…"I can't wait to do that again!"

Chapter 31
PROTECT OUR CRAGS

"You don't know what you've got til it's gone."
Joni Mitchell

In the early 1980s, I hand drilled a bolt on the roof of Triangulation, a new route I established at Quoddy Head State Park in northeastern Maine, when a 70-year-old ranger appeared at the base.

"What the hell do ya think you're doing?" he yelled with a thick Maine accent.

"I'm placing a bolt."

"I can see that," the ranger spat with a mouthful of tobacco. "But who gave ya permission?"

"I didn't know I needed permission."

So, I rappelled to the ground and explained how I was making the route safe for future climbers.

But the ranger did not want to hear it.

"That's all well and good," the ranger spat. "But as far as I'm concerned, you're forbidden to climb here without a permit."

I questioned whether such a requirement existed, but I knew my argument would not serve my best interest. I learned from Dan Inosanto, Bruce Lee's sparring partner, the highest level in martial arts is to avoid the fight in the first place - the true meaning of *Be like Water*.

"So, how do I go about getting a permit?" I asked.

"Ya have to go to Augusta," the ranger replied with a tobacco filled grin.

Augusta, the state's capital, was 4 hours away, but that was nothing to me. I had driven across the country more than a dozen times.

It was quarter to five when I arrived at the Park and Service office, and nobody was willing to help me. Permit applications were no longer accepted, and I had to return the next day. But I refused to take no for an answer.

I knocked on doors and talked to anyone willing to hear my case. When one person learned I was born and raised in Cape Porpoise, Maine, and a supporter of Senator George Mitchell, the proverbial seas parted. Within minutes I was issued a permit. You should have seen the look on the ranger's face when I returned the following day with a permit in my hand.

The ranger stared at the permit for nearly five minutes as if he couldn't believe his eyes. He instructed me to wait while he drove to his home and made a few calls to ensure the permit was legit.

I do not know what was said to him, but from that day forth, the ranger's attitude changed, and we became good friends, proving that being like water is the best way to be. Today, you can climb at Quoddy Head State Park without a permit, but please take this right seriously.

Legislators can restrict our rights with a stroke of the pen or a change of ownership, which is why we need to support nonprofit organizations like the Access Fund.

Since founded in 1990, the Access Fund has preserved more than 17,400 acres. From Jailhouse Rock and Donner Summit in California to the New River Gorge in West Virginia and Red River Gorge in Kentucky.

The Access Fund advocates on the climber's behalf to preserve access for generations to come. So, if you have the means, please donate to this incredible nonprofit organization. Not only will your donation be tax deductible, but it will make you feel like a contributing member of our climbing community. As Joni Mitchell warned...

"You don't know what you've got til it's gone."

Chapter 32
SUPPORT OUR RESCUE TEAMS

"So others can live."

SAR Motto

Quinn Brett was a world-class climber pursuing the women's speed climbing record on the Nose of El Capitan in Yosemite Valley, California. Quinn knew what was at stake when she ran it out on Boot Flake (Pitch 16), but she ran it out anyway.

Although the World's Most Dangerous Race (Listen to the Podcast) has never officially been a legitimate race with spectators, prize money, and a television network streaming the event live, every competitor knew that a slip-on Boot Flake could be a death fall. But Quinn was willing to take that risk.

The only thing that mattered was the record. Had Quinn slept the night before, she might have been in the proper mind space, but her thoughts were preoccupied with her two friends, Hayden Kennedy and Inge Perkins, who were killed in an avalanche day before in Montana.

Quinn thought of postponing their ascent until she was in a better head place, but she pushed those thoughts aside and decided to go for it anyway.

Then the unthinkable happened.

Quinn popped off.

Nobody knows who first climbed Boot Flake in this manner (not clipping or placing protection), but Hans Florine, the author of On the Nose, and former record holder with Alex Honnold, believes it may have been Dave Shultz or Peter Croft in 1990.

Shultz and Croft's ascent proved to be a game changer because it enabled the belayer to pendulum swing without needing to climb or clean the Boot Flake. Quinn used the same technique when she established the women's record in 2016, but as she plummeted through space without anything to impede her free fall, she wished she had listened to those whispers.

And so did Josie McKee.

As a former (YOSAR) Yosemite Search and Rescue team member, McKee had been Quinn's partner on numerous big wall ascents. They had perfected the art of simul-climbing together, but she had the same reservations before their ascent.

Now McKee wished she had listened.

As a YOSAR rescue team member, you are trained and prepared for most life-threatening situations, but nothing could prepare McKee for what was about to happen. Quinn flew by like a wing suit jumper gathering speed before pulling their chute.

Only Quinn didn't have a chute. She slammed into the Texas Flake at near terminal velocity speed.

KA-SLAM!

Quinn's helmet exploded on impact, then she tumbled behind the flake into a pile of rocks.

"QUINN!" Josie screamed.

But there was no response.

Why would there be?

Nobody could survive such a horrific fall. Trying not to panic, Josie called YOSAR on her cellphone, but nobody answered.

"Damn it!"

Josie knew better than to call 911, so she tried dispatch and was connected to Philip Johnson, the shift supervisor, who immediately authorized a helicopter rescue, and from that moment on the clock was ticking.

If Quinn was alive, she didn't have much time. Realizing the urgency, McKee quickly rappelled down to Quinn. Upon reaching her best friend, Josie heard Quinn gasping as if she had difficulty breathing, but the uncontrolled bleeding was Josie's most significant concern.

Quinn was bleeding out.

So, Josie up-righted Quinn, applied a tourniquet around her friend's head using her neck gaiter, and began administering emergency CPR.

"Stay with me Quinn. We are going to get you out."

But Quinn was drifting in and out of consciousness, and it was debatable whether she would live long enough to be evacuated. It is one thing to practice CPR in a classroom with a dummy; it's entirely another matter when you are on a 3,000-foot granite wall attempting to save your best friend.

If it hadn't been for McKee's decisive actions and the helicopter rescue, Quinn would have died. Three hours after receiving Josie's phone call, Quinn was airlifted to a medical facility by some of the bravest people you will ever meet and hope you will never need. But if you do....

You will be glad you have supported your local search and rescue teams. Because of YOSAR, Quinn and many others like her have survived. Quinn may be paralyzed from the waist down, but that does not mean she will be paralyzed forever with today's medical breakthroughs.

So, when considering a tax-deductible donation, place our search and rescue teams on your list, for without these courageous people continuously putting their lives on the line, our climbing community would not be free to push the limits. We just need to listen to those whispers better.

Chapter 33
PRAISE YOUR ROUTE SETTERS

"Setting routes is a labor of love."

Dan Goodwin

Setting routes is an art form and a labor of love. Nobody sets routes because they want to become rich and famous. Route setters set because they love to create movement, using the walls as their canvas and the holds as their paint. While we get to stand at the base and say...

"WOW! I can't wait to climb that."

When I began setting routes in the early 1980's on plywood walls with screw-on wood holds, I never thought I would be designing and constructing the world's tallest climbing wall in Snowbird, Utah (1988), for the First International Sport Climbing championship.

Talk about 'WOW!'

The idea was hatched the year before at the Outdoor Retailer Expo in Las Vegas. Wild Things from North Conway, New Hampshire, invited me to erect a climbing wall at their booth, directly across from Gore-Tex. The wall was a hit, even though nobody was allowed to climb it for liability reasons. I was beginning to wonder if anything would come from my efforts when Jeff Lowe, a renowned American alpinist, approached me.

"I heard your talk the other day," Lowe began. "You were predicting that climbing would be in the Olympics.

"Do you disagree?" I asked.

"Not at all," Lowe assured. "I just don't know about the timing, but I was wondering if you would like to collaborate on an idea I have."

"What idea is this?"

Jeff looked either way to make sure nobody was listening. "I would like to organize the world's first international climbing competition, and I was wondering if you would like to be involved."

I couldn't believe my luck. Lowe was the first accomplished climber to embrace my ideas since I launched Sport Climbing Systems, a climbing wall company with nearly 100 bolt-on holds and texture panels.

"Do you have a place in mind?" I replied.

"As a matter of fact I do. The Cliff Lodge at Snowbird, Utah."

I had climbed in Little Cottonwood Canyon a few years back, linking two pitches into one on <u>Fallen Arches 5.13b/c</u>. See photo.

So, I was familiar with the area.

"I am friends with Dick Bass," Lowe added. "The owner and first person to scale the tallest peak on all seven continents."

I heard about Dick Bass through Geoff Tabin, an accomplished alpinist and physician on a similar quest.

"Do you think he would be interested?" I asked.

"He would if you were involved," Lowe countered.

"Who will cover our expenses?"

"Dick Bass initially," Lowe assured. "He is a billionaire on paper, but most of our expenses will be covered through television rights."

"Do you have a network in mind?"

"As a matter of fact, I do," Lowe confessed. "I am good friends with a hot shot producer with CBS Sports. We just need a catchy title. Do you have any ideas?"

"Why don't we call it the First International Sport Climbing Championship," I suggested, playing off my company's name.

Dan Goodwin - Fallen Arches - Photo: Anne-Marie Weber

100

"I love it," Jeff resounded. "I'll pitch it to Bass and my friend with CBS."

And that my friends is how the competition came about, but as we quickly discovered, saying you are going to host the First International Sport Climbing Championship was one thing, constructing and setting up the routes on the ten-story wall with a large roof (made by different company) and dual speed routes was another.

For weeks, our team debated on how difficult the semi-finals and the finals should be. We failed miserably for the women's (our apologies), but we knocked it out of the park with the men. With only one competitor remaining, the entire audience was wondering if anyone would reach the top until Patrick Edlinger, the French superstar, captured one of the most dramatic ascents in televised history.

Of course, that is open for debate, but our climbing community owes the route setters a tremendous amount of gratitude. If it weren't for route setter's efforts, Sport Climbing might not have taken off. CBS Sports was not obligated to air the show if it wasn't exciting enough to captivate a non-climber audience.

So, next time you see the route setters hard at work, I pray you remember this chapter. Don't just walk by. Let these talented artists know how much you appreciate their efforts. Not only will your gratitude pump them up, but it will create the kind of vibe we all desire.

Chapter 34
BE SOCIAL MEDIA CONSCIOUS

"Fear leads to anger. Anger leads to hate.
Hate leads to suffering."

Yoda

The importance of online reputation management cannot be overstated in the current digital age. With the rise of social media platforms and online communication, individuals and businesses alike need to be aware of their digital footprint and how it can impact their reputation. Therefore, be mindful of what you post on social media; your words, images, or videos may return to haunt you.

A few years ago, a professional rock climber made derogatory remarks about a female climber's fluctuating body weight on his social media page.

Why this sponsored climber felt the need to make hurtful comments about a colleague is anyone's guess, but the response was swift. Within hours of his distasteful post, he was dropped by all his major sponsors, stating this athlete violated the company's core values.

So, as a rule, if you don't have anything good to say on social media, don't say it, even if your friends are engaging in the hate parade.

Resist the temptation.

Be the better person by refusing to participate. Use social media as an opportunity to be a uniter, not a divider. Focus on sharing climbing experiences or tips instead. You may feel this advice infringes on your freedom of speech, but most climbers will vehemently disagree if you demean a person we all revere. Be the person that praises others, not the other way around.

As Obi-Wan Kenobi warned...

"Beware of anger, fear, and aggression. The dark side are they. Once you start down the dark path, forever will it dominate your destiny."

Don't let this happen to you. We all know what happened with Darth Vader. So next time you are about to post a comment that may be deemed derogatory and hurtful, think twice. Nothing is worth losing your source of income or standing in our community. If you wish to debate issues, please do so, but stick to the <u>Golden Rule</u>.

Be cool!

Don't be the person that loses your cool because the moment you do, you have lost the debate. Be the one that displays inner peace and sets an example of how to engage civilly. If you take this chapter seriously, you will not only become an outstanding member of our community, but you will likely increase the number of people that will follow you on your social media.

How cool would that be?

MINDFULNESS

Chapter 35
DON'T JUDGE

*"When you judge others, you do not define them,
you define yourself."*

Earl Nightingale

Let's face it; nobody likes being around people who are always making derogatory remarks about other climbers. It makes you wonder if they are talking smack about you when you aren't around. Don't allow yourself to be one of them. It says more about you than it does about the person being judged.

So, as a rule, only say something if you have something good to say. Better yet, steer the conversation in another direction and praise another person's efforts instead. You will be amazed how it will affect everyone's attitude and the overall vibe. Be a motivator, not a total downer with nothing good to say. Just because someone cannot climb as hard or are not as physically fit or as lean as you does not mean this person is not extraordinary in other ways.

Everyone has a story. You may not know it, but that person could be dealing with a life-threatening illness, an injury, or a sixty-hour work week with a new baby, but you will never know if you pass judgment on them. It is important to treat each climber as an individual rather than making generalizations based on external factors.

Overcoming personal bias requires self-awareness and reflection. It involves acknowledging our own preconceptions and actively challenging them. This can be achieved by engaging in conversations with climbers from diverse backgrounds or seeking out experiences that challenge our beliefs.

Ultimately, overcoming personal bias allows us to create a more inclusive climbing community where all climbers are valued regardless of their background or identity. Which reminds me of a story.

There was once a businessman that purchased a package of chocolate chip cookies while waiting for a delayed flight out of Los Angeles. He took a seat at a communal table with his laptop computer and reached for a cookie from an opened package. But before he could grab one, a college student grabbed one from across the table and smiled.

"These are pretty good. Aren't they?"

The traveler couldn't believe his eyes. How dare this person take one of his cookies without asking. Not wishing to make a scene, he went back to his laptop and ate his cookie, shaking his head.

A few minutes later, the business man was about to reach for another cookie when the college student did the same, smiling and motioning to package as if saying "You should have an another."

Outraged, the businessman snatched another cookie from the package while mouthing these words. "What a nerve. Can anyone believe this guy?"

Begrudgingly the businessman ate his cookie and composed a text to his girlfriend about the incident. After sending the text, he looked up as the college student grabbed the last cookie.

You got to be kidding.

The businessman was going to say something when the college student did something unexpected, he split the cookie and handed him the larger piece. Before he could respond, the college student picked up the empty package, smiled, and gestured 'Goodbye' as he walked away with his carryon bag.

It was then the angry businessman saw an unopened package of cookies beneath his magazine. In that instance, he realized he'd been eating the other man's cookies all along.

Not the other way around.

How many times have you passed judgment on someone, only to realize later that you were wrong? Has it ever happened the other way around where you were being judged?

It doesn't feel good.

Does it?

So, as a rule, make a conscious effort to refrain from passing judgment on others. Let's learn from each other and grow as a community by celebrating our diversity. If you adopt this way of thinking, the odds of you making long-lasting friendships, and living a happy and fulfilling life will increase immensely.

Chapter 36
STOP COMPARING

"Comparing yourself is the thief of joy ."
Theodore Roosevelt

Comparing oneself to others can be a dangerous psychological game. Left unchecked, comparing oneself to other climbers or more successful people can be the gateway to feelings of inadequacy, low self-esteem, eating disorders, and depression.

Social media platforms like Instagram and Facebook are notorious for showcasing the highlight reels of people's lives. It's important to remember that what you see on social media is often not an accurate representation of reality.

When we focus too much on what others are doing, we lose sight of our own accomplishments and progress. It's important to remember that everyone's journey is different and success looks different for everyone.

Additionally, this mindset can create a toxic culture within the climbing community. Instead of celebrating each other's successes and supporting one another, it becomes a competition where only those who are the best are valued. This can lead to a lack of inclusivity and discourage newcomers from joining the community. Ultimately, it's important to focus on our own goals and progress instead of comparing ourselves to others.

We should celebrate our successes and support others in their journeys without feeling like we have to constantly measure up to someone else's standards. This will not only benefit our mental health but also create a more positive and inclusive climbing community.

Instead of comparing ourselves to others, let us focus on our own journey and find motivation within ourselves to reach new heights. Focusing on personal progress rather than external validation can have numerous benefits for climbers. When we compare ourselves to others, we often become consumed with jealousy, insecurity, and even a lack of motivation.

However, when we focus on our own progress, we can celebrate our small victories and enjoy the journey of climbing. By focusing on personal progress, we can develop a deeper understanding of our strengths and weaknesses. We can set realistic goals for ourselves and work towards achieving them without being distracted by what others are doing. This helps us to build confidence in our abilities, not only as a climber, but with everything else in life.

Chapter 37
STOP MAKING EXCUSES

"Ninety-nine percent of the failures come from people who have the habit of making excuses."
George Washington Carver

The negative effects of making excuses in climbing and life are numerous. When we make excuses, we limit ourselves and our potential for growth. In climbing, making excuses can prevent us from pushing ourselves to try harder routes or push through difficult moves. Excuses can also lead to a lack of progress and discourage us from continuing to climb altogether. In life, making excuses can prevent us from achieving our goals and living up to our full potential.

It can lead to missed opportunities and personal growth. Making excuses can also negatively impact relationships as it shows a lack of accountability and responsibility. Overall, making excuses is a self-defeating behavior that hinders progress both in climbing and in life. It is important to recognize when we are making excuses and take action.

Firstly, we need to set clear and achievable goals. We should write down our goals on a piece of paper and keep it somewhere visible. This will remind us of what we want to achieve and keep us motivated. Secondly, we need to identify the excuses that are holding us back. We should be honest with ourselves and ask why we make these excuses.

Once identified, we can work on ways to overcome them. Thirdly, we need to take action towards our goals every day. It's important to break down big goals into smaller ones and take small steps towards them each day.

Lastly, we need to surround ourselves with people who support our goals. Having a supportive community can make all the difference when it comes to achieving our dreams.

Making excuses or blaming others can lead to dangerous situations. Similarly, taking personal responsibility in life means accepting that our actions have consequences. It means recognizing that we have control over our choices and the outcomes they produce. Making excuses or blaming others only serves to limit our potential for growth and improvement. In both climbing and life, personal responsibility requires honesty with oneself.

You may have legitimate reasons for your disappointing performance. You could be dealing with an injury or not enough sleep but resist the temptation to make excuses because nobody wants to hear it, and neither do you.

Besides, making excuses have a way of becoming a self-fulfilling prophecy. We have all heard the phrase; what you think about, you bring about; making excuses falls into this category. If you want to reach your full potential, you must make a conscious effort to eliminate excuses from your vocabulary.

If you fail to send your route, do not waste your time making up excuses. Think of how you can approach the climb differently. There could be any number of reasons, and if you examine each, you may discover a clue as to what to do. Empower yourself with the belief you possess everything you need to succeed in this game of life and apply that to climbing.

When I first met Lynn Hill in the late 1970s in Joshua Tree National Park in southern California, Lynn was climbing with John Long and John Bachar.

Despite being the shortest, not once did Lynn use her height (5'2") as an excuse. Instead, Lynn would create her own beta and send the route or boulder with relative ease. I climbed with Lynn at Red Rock Canyons, then again at Smith Rocks, outside Bend, Oregon, belaying her on Churning in the Wake 5.13a.

Lynn was crushing it.

When I heard Lynn free climbed the Nose of El Capitan in Yosemite Valley, California in 1994, a feat not achieved by any other person, male or female, I wasn't the least bit surprised. Had Lynn used her height as an excuse, she would never have realized her true potential.

The same is true with Tommy Caldwell, who lost his left index finger in 2001, while working with a table saw. That accident could have ended Caldwell's climbing career, but he refused to listen to his physician, who didn't believe he would ever climb at the same level again. Imagine how that must have affected Caldwell's mind space. Most would have sunk into a deep depression, but not Tommy. He wasn't going to use his missing finger as an excuse.

Instead, Caldwell underwent months of rehabilitation until he was able to focus his attention on Dawn Wall on El Capitan in Yosemite Valley. Nobody thought the aid route could be free climbed, but Caldwell never stopped believing.

Four years later (January 14, 2015), Caldwell and his partner, Kevin Jorgeson, the bouldering phenomena, reached the summit. The ascent took 19 days, proving to themselves and the world, that anything is possible if you don't make excuses.

So, next time you are about to make an excuse, think of Lynn Hill and Tommy Caldwell. Not only will their shinning example help guide you on your climbing journey, but it will also make you a better person in the process.

Chapter 38
STOP CHASING THE GRADES

"Chasing the grades is like a dog chasing its tail.
Only the dog is having more fun."
Dan Goodwin

One of the reasons why you should stop chasing grades in climbing is to focus on enjoying the process of climbing. Many climbers become too fixated on achieving a certain grade or sending a particular route, that they forget to appreciate the journey and the experiences that come with it. Climbing is not just about reaching the top, but also about pushing yourself mentally and physically, problem-solving, and learning new skills.

When you focus too much on grades, you might miss out on trying new routes or styles that could challenge and improve your skills. You might also become discouraged if you don't send a route within your desired grade range. By shifting your focus to enjoying the process of climbing, you'll be able to appreciate each climb for what it is - an opportunity to learn something new or improve upon existing skills.

This mindset can help you find joy in even the smallest successes and motivate you to keep pushing yourself further without becoming too attached to grades. Ultimately, by enjoying the process of climbing, you'll find more fulfillment in this sport than simply chasing after grades.

It is okay to dream. Dreamers are the pioneers of the future, but if you become overly obsessed, you will forget to enjoy the journey. It is okay to have goals. I am the king of goal setting and charting courses of action, but I learned to keep my expectations in check.

Not all goals are worth pursuing, especially if the price exceeds what you are willing to pay. If you are climbing to have fun, then keep it fun. Keep your ego checked at the door. Do not put yourself in a life-threatening position because you are chasing the grades.

Here is a secret.

Most people don't care how hard you climb. Sure, they will be impressed by your abilities, but if you strut around with an attitude, thinking you are better than everyone else, most climbers will find that distasteful. Do not be that person. Be a person that is humble and mindful of others.

Remember, happiness is an inside job. You will never find happiness chasing the grades because there will always be a route that will shut you down. Those routes may give you a sense of purpose, motivation, and drive, but they can also be dangerous and destructive if left unchecked.

You may think this will never happen to you, but trust me, sooner or later, you will reach your peak, and you will no longer be able to send the routes you once did. When this happens, I hope you remember this chapter because the joy of climbing has nothing to do with the grades.

Chapter 39
TRUST the PROCESS

"Patience is a virtue."

Poet William Langland

Climbing has a steep learning curve. Strength gains require time. Any effort to speed up the process will yield nothing but frustration and injuries. Avoid this pitfall. When you trust the process you are not placing any timelines. It's okay to set goals but make sure your goals are realistic.

Otherwise, you will be setting yourself up for a world of frustration.

Think years.

Not days or weeks.

Sure, you can get hellaciously strong in four to six weeks, but imagine how strong you could get if you gave yourself four to six months.

Or a year.

Not only would you be more realistic with your expectations, but you will likely enjoy the process even more. The advice applies to injuries as well. Everyone hates being placed on the injured list but sooner or later, if you are pushing yourself, it will happen to you. When that happens, I hope you give yourself permission to trust the rehab process. Refrain from cutting your rehab short. The only person you will be shorting is you.

Chapter 40
REPLACE the WORD 'TAKE'

"Watch me."

Boone Speed

If I received a dollar each time I've heard someone yell '*Take*', I could pay off the national debt. Just joking, but you know what I mean. It seems like the word has become the most commonly used word in a climber's vocabulary.

But here is a secret.

If you want to take your climbing to a higher level, possessing the ability to flash or onsight routes, you should replace this word with...

'*WATCH ME!*"

When a lead climber uses these words, it means they could take a rip, and that you should get ready to catch them. When I was climbing at Smith Rocks in 1980s, I had the pleasure of watching Boone Speed onsight a few 5.12s. Every time he arrived at the crux, Boone would yell...

"*Watch me.*"

I never heard Boone utter the word '*Take*'. He fought for every clip like a featherweight fighter until he was doing the same on 5.13s and eventually 5.14s.

So, if you want to take your climbing to a new level, start replacing the word 'Take'. Not only will you convey a different message to your belayer, but your words will have a profound impact on your brain.

For what we think about, we bring about, and that is particularly true with climbing.

One word shuts you down.

Take!"

The other command fires you up.

"*Watch me!*"

If your goal is to send routes, get into a habit of fighting until the very end. Just watch a world cup bouldering or lead climbing video and you will see what I mean.

You will never hear them yell '*Take*.'

The only thing you will see are world class athletes gunning for the top or falling while lunging for the highest hold.

Working routes is great. It allows climbers to send route they couldn't do otherwise. But if you want to become a sending machine, flashing and on sighting routes on a regular basis, then you must embrace this mindset. And when you do, I hope you remember this chapter and give thanks to Boone Speed, who inspired me to do the same.

Chapter 41
MAKE FEAR YOUR ALLY

"Fear is my super power."

Dan Goodwin

Climbing can be an intense and exhilarating experience, but it can also be quite intimidating. Fear is a common emotion that many climbers experience when faced with challenging climbs or unfamiliar terrain. Understanding the psychology of fear in climbing is crucial if you want to make it your ally. Fear is a natural response to a perceived threat, and it can be helpful or harmful depending on how you respond to it.

In climbing, fear can keep you safe by alerting you to potential dangers, such as loose rocks or unstable footholds. However, if you let fear control you, it can paralyze your decision-making and lead to poor choices.

To use fear as an ally in climbing, it's important to recognize when your fear response is legitimate and when it's irrational. You can do this by practicing mindfulness and self-awareness. When you feel afraid while climbing, take a moment to assess the situation objectively. Is there really a danger present? Or are you simply feeling nervous because of the height or exposure?

Once you've identified what's causing your fear, work on developing strategies for managing it. This might involve breathing techniques, positive self-talk, visualization exercises or seeking support from other climbers. While fear can be paralyzing, it can also be a useful tool if we know how to use it. To make fear our ally in climbing, we need to develop effective strategies that help us manage our emotions and remain calm under pressure.

One technique is to focus on breathing. Slow, deep breaths can help regulate our heart rate and calm our mind. Another technique is positive self-talk. Repeating affirmations like "I am strong" or "I can do this" can help boost our confidence and reduce anxiety.

By focusing on positive thoughts, you can shift your mindset from one of fear to one of confidence and determination.

Visualization is another powerful tool that climbers use to manage their fears. By picturing yourself successfully completing the climb before actually attempting it, you can mentally prepare yourself for the challenge ahead.

Another way to address your fears is by starting with easier climbs before tackling more challenging routes. This will allow you to gradually gain confidence and experience without overwhelming yourself with fear. If something doesn't feel right or safe, don't hesitate to speak up or take a step back.

By building trust in yourself and your equipment, you can turn fear into an ally that helps you stay focused and alert while climbing.

Practicing falling in a controlled and safe environment is another recommended way to help you address your fears. Whatever approach you choose, remember that overcoming fear takes practice and patience. By developing strong mental strategies and building your confidence over time, you can become a more fearless climber.

However, fear can also have some surprising physiological effects on the body during climbing that can actually enhance our performance. When we experience fear, the body releases adrenaline and other stress hormones that increase heart rate, blood pressure, and respiration. This physiological response prepares us for a fight or flight response and sends more oxygen-rich blood to our muscles.

This surge of energy can give climbers an extra boost of strength and endurance that they may not have had otherwise. Additionally, fear can sharpen our focus and improve our reaction time as we become hyper-aware of our surroundings. This heightened state of alertness allows climbers to make split-second decisions and react quickly in dangerous situations.

Many climbers have used fear to their advantage, pushing past their limits and achieving extraordinary feats. One example is Alex Honnold, who made history by free soloing El Capitan in Yosemite National Park. Honnold's fear of falling drove him to meticulously plan and train for the climb, allowing him to execute it flawlessly despite the immense risk involved.

Similarly, Lynn Hill used her fear of failure to become the first person ever to free climb The Nose on El Capitan.

So, next time you're dealing with this powerful emotion, try using fear to help you send. It may take a moment for the adrenaline and endorphins to kick in; but, if you hang with it and continue charging as if your life depends on it, you may experience a surge of strength as Lynn Hill and Alex Honnold did.

Chapter 42
BE A ROCK WARRIOR

*"A rock warrior never gives up.
They only try harder!"*

Dan Goodwin

In the ancient times, there existed a tribe of warriors who were known as the rock warriors. They were renowned for their immense strength and resilience in battle. These warriors lived in mountainous regions and were trained to fight using rocks and boulders as their primary weapons.

The rock warriors were a highly disciplined group of fighters who would spend hours each day practicing their combat skills. They believed that strength and skill could only be acquired through hard work and dedication, so they took their training very seriously.

The rock warriors may be long gone, but their spirit lives on in the hearts of all those who seek strength and resilience in the face of adversity. In conclusion, the story of the rock warriors is one of strength, discipline, and respect for nature. They were fierce fighters who lived their lives with honor and dignity. Their legacy serves as an inspiration to all those who seek to overcome challenges and achieve greatness through hard work and dedication.

However, even today, there are those who seek out the teachings and ways of the rock warriors. Their strength, resilience, discipline, respect for nature, spirituality, artistry and thirst for knowledge still resonate with many people today who seek inspiration from ancient cultures that lived close with nature.

The rock warriors may have been a long forgotten tribe, but their impact on the world is still felt today by those who seek to learn from the wisdom of the past.

To become a rock warrior, one must undergo both physical and mental training. The physical aspect is crucial, as climbing requires a great deal of strength and endurance. Climbers must build up their upper body strength through exercises such as pull-ups and hang boards, as well as increase their flexibility and balance through stretches and yoga.

Mental training is equally important for climbers. They must learn to control their fear and remain calm in stressful situations. This can be achieved through visualization techniques and meditation.

Becoming a rock warrior takes time, dedication, and discipline. It requires pushing oneself out of comfort zones both physically and mentally while constantly learning a new skill. Every climber gets intimidated, but a rock warrior knows our true potential is just outside our comfort zone.

The key is believing and not beating yourself up for past mistakes. If you are going to believe in something, believe in yourself. Believing is the first step in achieving.

The biggest mistake a climber can make is to gauge their happiness and self-worth on their most recent ascent. It's okay to be happy about our achievements; we should always celebrate those moments but also strive to enjoy the journey and cherish each moment as if it were our last.

A rock warrior embraces this way of thinking as a way of life, knowing there is no better moment than the here and now.

Chapter 43
PAY IT FORWARD

"Always dream of the impossible, then try!"
Geoff Tabin

The concept and philosophy behind "paying it forward" are based on doing good deeds for others without expecting anything in return. The phrase "pay it forward" means to repay a good act done to you by doing a good deed for someone else, creating a chain reaction of kindness. This simple yet powerful concept encourages individuals to be mindful of how they can positively impact the lives of others.

Paying it forward can take many forms, from acts of kindness like opening the door for someone to volunteering your time or donating money to charity. Regardless of the scale, every act of kindness can make a difference in someone's life and contribute to a more compassionate and connected community.

The concept and philosophy behind paying it forward remind us that we are all connected and that even small actions can significantly impact us. There are numerous examples of organizations, communities, and individuals who practice paying it forward.

Dr. Geoff Tabin is one.

We met in Black Velvet Canyon in Red Rock National Park, near Las Vegas, when I established the first ascent of Ixtlan 5.11c with George and Joanne Urioste.

It was 1980.

Interest rates were 13.5%, unemployment was 7.5%, and John Lennon was dead, gunned down by a madman outside his New York home, but we weren't interested in talking about things we could not change. We were only interested in climbing.

Not only was Tabin a medical student at Harvard, but he also seemed hellbent on getting a doctorate in climbing by taking advantage of promotional flights from Boston, which offered three nights at a casino hotel plus a $50 voucher for chips.

However, it would be three years before we saw each other again. This time, it was at Devil's Lake, Wisconsin. I was conducting a workshop titled '*Master Your Fears*' with a dozen martial artists from the Fred Degerberg Academy in Chicago.

All my students feared heights, so I demonstrated the power of the mind by free soloing Bagatelle, 5.12d. That is when I learned Tabin intended to scale the unclimbed East Face of Everest. We even talked about climbing together upon his return, but neither realized how much our lives would change.

After scaling Everest, one of the seven tallest peaks on each continent - which Tabin would later climb, he encountered a Dutch medical team conducting a cataract surgery on a Tibetan woman who had been blind for three years.

That experience was so transformational that Tabin decided to devote his life to curing people who were blind. But as we all know, saying you will do something and doing it are often worlds apart, but Dr. Tabin remained true to his word by returning to Nepal to work with Dr. Sanduk Ruit, hailed as the 'God of Sight' to the world's poor.

Together, the two eye surgeons co-founded the Himalayan Cataract Project (HCP), a non-profit organization working to eradicate preventable blindness in the developing world.

Since its inception in 1995, the Himalayan Cataract Project has provided free eye care to over one million people and performed over 200,000 sight-restoring surgeries in many of the poorest and most remote regions, such as Ethiopia and Rwanda.

This act of kindness and generosity earned Dr. Tabin the prestigious Dalai Lama award as the 'Unsung Hero'!

When asked if he intended to retire, Dr. Tabin shook his head and smiled.

"No. I'm just getting started."

Today, Dr. Tabin teaches and travels the globe with his wife, Dr. In-hei Hahn, training surgeons on his cataract removal techniques in partnership with Stanford University in Palo Alto, California.

You may wonder what you can do to pay it forward. Giving this book to a friend can be one. Donating to a non-profit organization such as CureBlindness.org is yet another.

As for myself, I'm hoping this book will serve as my way of paying it forward for generations to come. If you enjoy great films, watch Pay it Forward. It will make you wonder what you can do.

PRO CLIMBING TIPS

Chapter 44
FIND A MENTOR

"One of the greatest values of mentors is the ability to see ahead what others cannot see and to help them navigate a course to their destination."
John Maxwell

Finding a mentor for climbing can be a game-changer for anyone looking to take their skills to the next level. The benefits of having a mentor are numerous and go beyond just improving one's climbing technique. A mentor can provide guidance, support, and motivation that is invaluable in the pursuit of becoming a better climber. One of the primary benefits of having a mentor is the ability to learn from someone who has more experience and knowledge in the sport. This fact may seem like a no-brainer, but you will be amazed at how tempting it will be to climb with people less capable than you just to make you feel better about yourself.

Beware of this trap.

A mentor can help climbers identify their strengths and weaknesses and provide specific feedback on how to improve. They can also teach climbers new techniques and strategies for tackling different types of routes or problems.

When I studied martial arts with the Dan Inosanto, a Jeet Kune Do grandmaster and sparring partner of the late Bruce Lee, I thought I would be learning how to fight like in the movie, The Game of Death. Instead, I learned how to *'Be like Water.'*

Imagine my surprise when Inosanto said, "The highest level in martial arts is not the black belt; it is about avoiding the fight in the first place."

And just like that, I understood the meaning. Instead of pushing back against resistance, attempting to defeat it, you pivot and roll like in basketball or football (soccer). You may wonder what this has to do with climbing, but as I discovered, this way of thinking has everything to do with climbing. My capabilities didn't approve just a letter grade; my abilities shot up a number grade.

That spring (May/1983), I free soloed, Bagatelle, 5.12d at Devil's Lake, Wisconsin. You may think you don't need a mentor, but if you are climbing with someone better than you, you may have sought one without realizing it.

When Chris Sharma was 15, rapidly becoming the world's best climber, he wasn't sure what the future looked like until he teamed up with Boone Speed, a sport photographer with an impressive list of hard sends to his name.

Boone had been working on a project known as 'Necessary Evil' in the Virgin River Gorge. Boone knew he couldn't do it, but he believed Sharma could. As it turned out, 'Necessary Evil' became Sharma's launching pad.

Nearly every first ascent afterwards was considerably harder. *Imagination*' in Ceuse, France, became the world's first 5.15a.

'Jumbo Love' on Clark Mountain in the Mojave National Preserve, California, became the first 5.15b.

But Sharma was searching for a route that was even harder. That's when Sharma discovered *La Dura Dura* (The Hard Hard) in Oliana, Spain.

When Sharma bolted the route, he didn't know if it would go, and for a while, Sharma had given up hope until he met Adam Ondra. Even though Ondra was younger than Sharma, Ondra had something that he needed; the motivation and belief he could do it.

Over the next two years, Sharma and Ondra worked on La Dura Dura, taking turns belaying each other. If you were an observer, you might have gotten the impression they were competing, but what they were doing was feeding off each other's energy. Then the impossible happened.

On February 23, 2013, Adam captured the first ascent of La Dura Dura, the world's first 5.15c (9b+). Instead of feeling depressed, Sharma felt happy for Ondra and relieved because the pressure was no longer on him.

And that's when Sharma became like water. He was no longer doing battle; he was at peace. So, when you find yourself unable to reach the next level, you may want to seek a mentor.

You will be glad you did.

Chapter 45
FOCUS ON YOUR FEET

"The key to climbing is focusing on your feet."
Jimmie Dunn

I took my first climbing lesson with the legendary Jimmie Dunn at Cathedral Ledge in North Conway, New Hampshire. I knew nothing about Jimmie other than witnessing him take a whipper on The Prow, while running along the base.

"Falling!"

I ducked and looked up, thinking someone was falling to their death. Only to see Jimmie bouncing mid-air by a rope attached to his harness.

"Damn it. I almost had it," Jimmie exclaimed.

Instead of making an excuse, Jimmie pulled himself back in, then sent the route cleanly. I didn't know anything about climbing. My only experience was climbing oak and maple trees, but Jimmie's warrior-like attitude spoke to me. And just like that, I wanted to become a climber.

So, I sprinted to the summit and asked Jimmie if he would teach me. Little did I know that experience would shape my life forever. The following day, Jimmie emerged from his VW van barefoot.

At first, I thought nothing of it because I was barefoot half the time, but I expected he would slip on a pair of shoes or sandals at one point. But Jimmie didn't do either. He retrieved a pack and a well-used rope and slammed the side door.

"Are you ready?" Jimmie asked.

Ten minutes later, we were standing at the base of a granite cliff. Jimmie uncoiled the rope and tied one end around his waist.

"Now, the thing you need to know about climbing is, it's all about your feet. Which is why I want you to climb this route barefoot. It will force you to focus on your feet."

Before I could respond, Jimmie free-soloed the route, set up the anchors, then rappelled back down.

"Now, it's your turn," Jimmie instructed. "As I said, just focus on your feet."

I looked up at the route and flashed on a Kung Fu TV scene where a Shaolin priest walked on a bed of rice paper without leaving a trace.

"In fact," Jimmie added. "When you place your toe, I want you to project this thought, "foot stick!'

"Foot stick," I repeated.

"Exactly," Jimmie assured.

I felt silly at first, but as I progressed upward, repeating this phrase (foot stick) inside my head, I realized the true definition of what you think about you bring about.

Foot stick!

I was not saying, *'Foot slip!'*

Five years later, I free-soloed Mickey's Beach Crack 5.12b in northern California for national TV. But what most people don't know, I led the route barefoot before my free solo to be sure of my footwork.

Now, I'm not suggesting you climb barefoot. Although, it might give you a deeper appreciation of today's shoes. In the old days, climbing shoes were stiff and flat like a pair of bowling shoes.

Today's shoes are downturned and are designed to give you pinpoint accuracy. If you want to understand how your shoes work, which I recommend downsizing (1/2 to full size) for a tighter fit, press the toe against the wall and pretend you are stepping on your big toe.

See how your shoes stick like glue?

Pretty cool, huh?

Now pivot the heel to the right and left without easing up on the pressure. Now you know how the pros can quickly drop their knee and smear against the climbing wall. These athletes are tapping into the mechanics of today's climbing shoes.

Bottom line....

If you learn how you use your feet, there will be no limit to what you can send, and that my friend is my wish for you.

Dan Goodwin - Mickey's Beach Crack - Anne-Marie Weber

Chapter 46
MASTER TOE & HEEL HOOKING

"When you toe & heel hook, it's like having another arm."
Unknown

Toe and heel hooking are two essential techniques in climbing that involve using the toes and heels of your shoes. Toe hooking is when you use the front part of your shoe to hook a hold, while heel hooking involves using the cup of your shoe to grip a hold.

These techniques are useful when climbing overhangs or steep walls where traditional handholds may not be enough. Toe and heel hooking can help you mantle, maintain balance, increase reach, and reduce strain on your arms. To perform a toe or heel hook, it's important to have strong hamstring muscles and good technique.

Start by positioning your foot correctly before pressing or squeezing with your leg muscles. Make sure to engage your core and keep your body close to the wall for maximum stability. Knowing when to use either technique in different climbing situations can be a game changer.

Mastering these techniques requires practice, but they can greatly improve your climbing and open up new routes for you to conquer. When you watch world cup climbers compete, you will notice how they toe and heel hook everything to maintain their balance.

But climber be warned.

Heel hooking is hamstring intensive. When your legs are fully engaged, the tension can strain your hamstring muscles and set you back for weeks, especially if you haven't warmed up properly or you haven't incorporated weight training exercises like hamstring curls and squats.

But if performed properly, heel hooks can be as useful as another arm. The key is the heel placement.

Be precise.

Don't just place your heel and think that's all you have to do. Look for an indentation and strategically place your heel and press downward while pointing your toe. Not only will this method of climbing enable you to clip, but it will allow you to reach above your head and grab a hold.

The same is true with toe hooks. When searching for a way to balance yourself, look for something to hook your toe. Toe hooks can be as useful as a side-pull and an excellent way to shake out and rest.

So, next time you are struggling to clip, reach a hold or rest, survey your surroundings and see if you can incorporate a toe or heel hook. Odds are you will find one. And when you do, I hope you remember this chapter and you will know what to do.

Chapter 47
BECOME A KNEE BAR MASTER

"Doing kneebars isn't about the length of your leg or wearing kneepads, it is a skill."
Adam Ondra

As a climber, you may have heard of the knee bar, but do you know what it is and how it works? A knee bar is a technique used to rest while climbing by wedging your knee beneath an overhang or a large hold. This allows you to take weight off your hands and arms, giving them a much-needed break. Knee bars are often used in overhanging routes where climbers need to conserve energy during long climbs.

One of the main benefits of using knee bars is that they allow climbers to take a break from using their arms and hands. By utilizing the strength of their legs and core instead, climbers are able to conserve energy and continue climbing for longer periods of time. Mastering knee bars requires practice and experience with different types of routes. When attempting knee bars, there are several common mistakes that climbers make.

Firstly, it's important to avoid relying solely on the knee bar to hold your weight. Instead, use it as a tool to redistribute your weight and allow for more efficient movement.

Secondly, be mindful of the position of your foot when setting up the knee bar. If your foot is too low or too high, it can cause discomfort and instability. Ensure that your foot is in a comfortable and secure position before committing to the knee bar.

Another mistake to avoid is overusing knee bars in situations where they may not be necessary or effective. Knee bars can be a useful technique, but they are not always the best option for every climb. It's important to assess each situation carefully and determine if a knee bar will truly benefit you or if there is another technique that would be more effective. A strategically placed knee bar can enable the climber to shake out, sometimes hands free, or grab a hold that was out of reach, or make a seemingly impossible clip.

Knee bars have become so important, it's questionable whether Adam Ondra, arguably one of the best climbers in the world, would have captured the first ascent of Silence 5.15d/9c, an overhanging sport route in Flatanger, Norway.

You may think knee barring is a form of cheating, but I assure you, this advance technique is used by all the world cup climbers. And if you want to take knee bars to a higher level, try wearing velcro knee pads. Not only will they save your legs, but these climbing specific products will also provide the same friction as your shoes.

So, the next time you see an opportunity to knee bar, cease it and start sending routes like Adam Ondra.

Chapter 48
MASTER the DEAD POINT

"Those that master the dead point will master climbing."
Dan Goodwin

One of the best kept secrets in climbing is the dead point. Dead pointing refers to the act of reaching for a hold that is out of reach. The dynamic movement requires coordination, timing, and precision. However, many climbers make the mistakes of not committing fully to the move. When attempting a dead point, climbers often hesitate or hold back instead of committing fully to the move.

If you release too soon, you will come up short. If you release too late, gravity will win the day after you overshoot the hold. That is why timing is everything. You need to release at the apex of your upward momentum. At that precise moment, you are no longer projecting upward, and you haven't yet started downward, giving you a brief opportunity to latch the hold without gravity interfering.

John Gill was master of dead pointing. As a former gymnast and professor of mathematics at the University of Southern Colorado, Gill understood the laws of gravity and motion better than most.

I was introduced to dead pointing in the late 1970s while bouldering in Joshua Tree National Park with the late John Bachar and John Long.

One boulder on their circuit was White Rastafaria (see photo), the most intimidating V2 highball problem you will ever stand underneath.

So, boulderers beware.

This overhung boulder is not for the light of heart because it requires a very committing, dead-point maneuver about halfway up with a nasty-looking boulder directly underneath. If you fell, you could easily break an ankle or back, even with a crash pad.

But we didn't have crash pads then.

When I watched Bachar and Long send the problem with relative ease, I knew better than to believe the same would be true with me. These Valley Boys were the masters of dead pointing, and I was a student searching for knowledge.

White Rastafaria was my initiation.

If I succeeded, I could continue along their circuit. If I failed, I would be carted away with a broken ankle. So, I knew what was at stake. I'm sure peer pressure and the boulder underneath provided the necessary incentive (I was scared shitless). Still, I learned a valuable lesson that has remained with me today, 40-plus years later.

So, master the dead point my friends and watch your climbing get taken to a higher level. That is my wish for you.

141

Dan Goodwin - White Rasterfaria - Photo by Anne-Marie Weber

Chapter 49
FOCUS ON YOUR BREATH

"Nothing calms my mind more than focusing on my breath"
Dan Goodwin

The importance of breathing in climbing cannot be understated. When climbing, your body requires a steady flow of oxygen to maintain its energy levels and endurance. Proper breathing techniques help ensure that you are getting the necessary amount of oxygen to your muscles. It's essential to focus on your breathing when climbing, as it can help you stay calm and focused. Not only does it help you climb more efficiently, but it also helps in reducing fatigue and increasing endurance.

Here are some tips on how to develop proper breathing habits: Firstly, focus on taking deep breaths from your diaphragm rather than shallow breaths from your chest. This allows for a greater intake of oxygen and better circulation throughout the body.

Secondly, try to synchronize your breathing with your movements while climbing. For instance, inhale as you reach up for a hold and exhale as you release tension. Thirdly, practice controlled breathing exercises such as meditation or yoga to improve lung capacity and control over one's breath. Lastly, make sure to stay hydrated before and during climbing sessions as dehydration can affect one's breathing.

Incorporating these techniques into your climbing routine will not only improve your overall performance but also enhance the overall experience of climbing itself.

Remember to take deep breaths and focus on the present moment while climbing! Focusing on your breath during a climb can have numerous benefits.

Firstly, it can help regulate your heart rate and prevent you from feeling overwhelmed or anxious. By taking deep, controlled breaths, you can maintain a steady pace and avoid hyperventilating or feeling lightheaded. Additionally, focusing on your breath can help improve your concentration and mindfulness, allowing you to stay present in the moment and fully engage with the climb.

This increased focus can also help you make better decisions about the sequence of moves and safety precautions. In situations where the climb is particularly challenging or requires significant physical exertion, focusing on your breath can also provide a source of motivation and mental strength to push through difficult sections.

One mistake climbers make is holding their breath while making a move. This can lead to oxygen deprivation and cause dizziness or even loss of consciousness. Another mistake is taking short, shallow breathes. This can lead to hyperventilation and fatigue.

It's important for climbers to focus on deep belly breathing, inhaling through the nose and exhaling through the mouth. This technique helps to increase oxygen intake and reduce tension in the body.

Climbers should also be aware of their breath during moments of stress or fear, such as when making a difficult move or feeling exposed on a route. Taking deep breaths can help calm the mind and reduce anxiety. When you focus on your breathing, you can improve your endurance and stay calm and relaxed while climbing.

To sync your breath with your movements, start by taking a deep breath before making each move. As you exhale, make the move and then inhale again before making the next move.

This helps to ensure that you are not holding your breath during difficult moves, which can cause tension and lead to fatigue.

Another technique is to count your breaths as you climb. This helps to keep you focused on the present moment and prevents distracting thoughts from entering your mind. Counting also helps to regulate your breathing so that it becomes more controlled and efficient.

When I scaled both sides of the <u>CN Tower in Toronto, Canada</u>, the winds were howling. On the east side I didn't feel it because I was sheltered by the towering concrete structure, but when I ran to the other side, I could see a massive Canadian flag flapping in the wind like a tethered bullwhip.

"Do you still want to climb both sides?" the representative for the tower asked.

"I'll be fine," I replied. "Does anyone have the time?"

I just free soloed the eastern side in 58 minutes (top of elevator shaft), and my intention was to complete both sides in 2 hours or less. But as I free soloed the western side with the Guiness Book of World Records as a witness, I was wondering if I had made a mistake.

KA-SLAP!

As the flag snapped meters above my head, I focused on my breathing, incorporating the techniques in this book. But what most people didn't know, I was also using my breath to propel me, a trick I learned from martial arts. Instead of holding my breath when reaching for a hold, I exhaled. When you exhale you are releasing expended energy. That was my technique when I blasted by the Canadian flag and tagged the top of the elevator shaft for a combined time of 2 hours. I was focused on my breath. And I'm inviting you to do the same.

Dan Goodwin - Photo by Anne-Marie Weber

Chapter 50
TAKE TIME to TRAIN
"The fittest athletes always rule the day!"
Dan Goodwin

Physical preparation is a crucial aspect of climbing that should not be ignored. Climbing demands a lot from the body, and it is essential to train the muscles to handle the stress that comes with it. This includes your forearms, biceps, triceps, and shoulders. Strengthening these muscles will help you climb more effectively and reduce the risk of injury.

To prevent injuries, it's important to warm up properly before climbing and to gradually increase the intensity of your workouts over time. By taking the time to train properly and focusing on injury prevention and recovery strategies, you can improve your performance as a climber while minimizing the risk of injury.

Goal-setting and tracking progress in climbing training are essential elements in developing a successful climbing routine. Setting achievable goals helps you stay focused, motivated, and committed to the training process.

Start by identifying your long-term goals, such as completing a particular climb or improving your overall technique. Break these goals down into smaller, more manageable short-term goals that can be achieved within a realistic timeframe.

Tracking your progress is equally important. It allows you to monitor how far you have come and identify areas where you need to improve. Use technology to help track your progress with apps or wearable devices that monitor heart rate, calories burned, and distance climbed.

This data can provide valuable insights into what works best for you and where changes need to be made. Below is a list of climbing specific exercises that will help you take your game to a higher level.

Lap Days

Pick a route within your ability but challenging enough after the second or third lap you might not be able to send. This is one of the most effective ways of building endurance and learning how to clip when your forearms are about to explode.

Ten - 5.10's.

Or eleven - 5.11's.

Or twelve - 5.12s.

You get the picture. The number grade doesn't matter, providing you are sending an equal number of letter grades (a, b, c, d) before proceeding to the next level. If you can do ten - 5.10s, you may want to add a few 5.11s until you can do eleven - 5.11s. Pro-Tip: This is a fantastic way to train for multi-pitch routes.

Traversing

Traversing is one of the most effective ways to train to failure. My favorite is the 80' traverse in Joshua Tree National Park known as Gun Smoke. The V3 traverse packs a punch, thus earning its name and reputation.

Pyramid Pull Ups

Here is how to play with two more people. The first person does a pull-up, then the rest of group does the same. Then the first person does two pull-ups and process continues until no one can increase the number of reps. If you can take it to 10 and back down, you will have completed 100 pull-ups.

Eldorados

This exercise should only be performed by experienced climbers because it can place a lot of stress on the elbows. However, if performed properly, this exercise can be one of the most effective ways of mastering the lock off. To perform an Eldorado, the climber does a complete pull-up, holds it, then moves to the right, and then to left while maintaining the lock off.

Rope Climbing

Rope climbing is a gymnast favorite. Not only does this exercise increase your grip strength, it will nuke your forearms, triceps, shoulders, and core if you maintain a pike position with your feet pointed, both on the ascent and descent.

Bachar Ladder

Invented by the late John Bachar, nothing will train you more for lock offs than a Bachar Ladder. But be warned, if not performed properly, this exercise can blow your elbows as it did Jerry Moffat. So, climber be warned.

Campus Board

Created by the late <u>Wolfgang Gullich</u> in 1988 to prepare for a route known as <u>Action Directe</u>, the campus board provides yet another way to train. But a word of caution; campus board training can be hazardous to your finger joints if you aren't warmed up properly. And even then, campus board training should only be utilized once per week, but shouldn't be included in your program unless you have one or two years climbing experience.

Hang Boards

When I began climbing in the late 1970s, hang boards didn't exist. So, I hung from the door jams (10 seconds on/10 seconds off) until I could no longer support my weight. Not only did this training exercise make my fingers insanely strong, but it also taught me how to perform a front lever.

149

Dan Goodwin - Photo by Anne-Marie Weber

Spray Wall is a short climbing wall with a zillion holds placed in a random order, enabling the climber to create their own routes.

Interactive Climbing Walls: A.k.a. SICTBs (standardized interactive climbing training boards).

1) **Kilter Board**. Invented in the late 1990s by Ian Powell and Jackie Hueftle. These 12' high training walls are adjustable and equipped with an interactive app and a LED light system that illuminates the holds to indicate the selected route.

2) **Moon Board.** Invented in 2004 by Ben Moon, this training wall with small holds is best suited for elite climbers due to the risk of injury.

3) **Grasshopper**. Founded by Boone Speed and engineer Jeremy Huckins, this adjustable wall is much like the Kilter Board, only more futuristic (if the rumors hold true) by incorporating a built in computer that will automatically adjust the angle to mimic a project.

Core Training.

If you want to take your climbing to a higher level without risk of injury, start incorporating core training into your daily routine.

1) **Leg Lifts**. Perform this exercise while hanging from a pull-up bar. In a controlled manner, slowly raise your legs to waist level or higher and hold it as long as you can. Then lower your legs in a controlled manner and repeat.

2) **Planks**. Considered the safest (if you have back issues) for strengthening your core. Simply get into a pushup position with your back straight and hold for 2 minutes or more. If you want to take the stress off your shoulders, simply perform this exercise on your elbows with a foam pad.

3) **Front Levers**. If you are looking for the ultimate core training exercise it is the front lever, which can be performed on a pull up bar, gymnastic rings, or a hang board. Bottom line, a dedicated training program is the gateway to building strength and endurance for harder routes. So, the next time you walk by one of these training devises, remember this chapter and check them out. You will be glad you did.

Dan Goodwin performing Front Lever

Chapter 51
BE MORE FLEXIBLE
"What's your secret."

Shiva Rae

The importance of flexibility for climbing performance cannot be overstated. Climbing requires a full range of motion in your joints and muscles, and without flexibility, you may struggle to make certain moves or reach certain holds. Additionally, being flexible can help prevent injury while climbing.

To improve your flexibility for climbing, it's important to incorporate stretching into your regular routine. Focus on stretches that target the muscles you use most often while climbing, such as your shoulders, hips, and hamstrings.

It's important to note that while stretching is crucial for improving flexibility, it should not be done immediately before climbing. Instead, stretch after a warm-up or at the end of a session to help prevent injury and improve recovery time.

As a climber, being flexible is vital for success. Stretching increases blood flow to your muscles, which helps to reduce the risk of injury and fatigue during climbs. It also helps to improve your range of motion, making it easier to reach high holds or make difficult moves.

Mobility exercises are also essential for climbers as they focus on specific movements that mimic climbing positions. These exercises help to improve joint stability and strengthen the muscles needed for climbing.

For example, mobility exercises that target the hips can help with high-stepping moves, while exercises that work on shoulder mobility can help with reaching overhead holds.

Incorporating stretching and mobility exercises into your training routine will not only make you a better climber but will also help prevent injuries and keep you climbing for years to come.

So next time you hit the gym or crag, make sure you take some time to warm-up with some stretches and add in some targeted mobility work into your routine. But remember to warm up before stretching and listen to your body's limits to prevent injury.

One approach is to dedicate a specific time to stretching before and after climbing sessions. This can involve performing dynamic stretches, such as leg swings and arm circles, to warm up the muscles before climbing. After climbing, static stretches like holding a lunge or hamstring stretch can be beneficial in reducing muscle tension.

Another strategy is to integrate yoga into the training routine. Yoga poses such as downward dog, pigeon pose, and warrior pose are excellent for increasing flexibility in key areas for climbers like hips and shoulders. It's also important to listen to your body and stretch accordingly.

The risks of overstretching or underestimating the importance of flexibility in climbing can lead to severe injuries that could have been easily avoided. Overstretching can result in muscle strain, while underestimating the importance of flexibility can lead to decreased mobility and range of motion. It is crucial to strike a balance between stretching enough and not pushing your body too far.

I admit, I am not the most flexible person on earth, but I have never stopped stretching because I know the importance of flexibility. In 2018, I participated in the <u>Wanderlust yoga festival</u> at Squaw Valley, California, for the 3rd year in a row with my darling wife, Cynthia Ado.

<u>Shiva Rae</u> was our favorite teacher. However, due to Shiva's popularity, her classes were held in an open tent large enough for a hundred students. I purposely positioned myself in the center to avoid drawing attention to my lack of flexibility, but when Shiva Rae took the stage, she scanned the sea of faces and looked straight at me. Then she jumped down from the stage, waded through the outstretched yoga mats and plopped herself in front of me, as if she knew I was the one student that needed this lesson. I thought I would die.

Had my darling wife not been at my side, I might have fled like the cowardly lion in the Wizard of Oz, but I chose to remain because I knew I had to face my worst fears (humiliation) and make my weakness (lack of flexibility) my greatest strength.

And I'm glad I did. You may think flexibility is overrated, but as the climbing grades become increasingly more challenging, flexibility will play a key role in performing high steps, heel hooks, splits, and preventing injuries.

Thirty minutes into Shiva Rae's routine, she demonstrated a more challenging posture; the foot behind the head pose. I wasn't sure what to do.

Is this a good time to make my escape?

But everyone's eyes were fixed on me, especially Shiva Rae. I glanced to either side to see if anyone else was as concerned as me, but they were all striking the pose as if it was their daily routine.

So, I tried.

Unfortunately, I couldn't get my foot behind my head. I was stuck with my foot only a few inches above my shoulder, using every ounce of strength I had to hold it there. And that's when Shiva Rae asked...

"What's your secret?"

It was so obvious Shiva was addressing me that the entire class burst out laughing, especially when I exploded out of the stance like a coiled spring. If I could have crawled into a hole, I would have done so, but I sat in a half-lotus instead and smiled. Judging by Shiva Rae's response, that was the answer she was seeking. I was the least flexible person in the class, but I didn't let that phase me.

And that was my secret.

Being flexible isn't just about striking beautiful mind-blowing poses; it's about having a flexible mind. Rigid thoughts lead to insecurity and low self-esteem, which will not only impact your climbing, but everything else in life. So, be flexible, my friends. Flexibility is the key to excellent health, financial wealth, and happiness, and it will help you send.

Chapter 52
TAKE RECOVERY TIME SERIOUSLY

"Resting is just as important as training."
Dan Goodwin

The importance of rest and recovery in climbing cannot be overstated. Climbing is a physically demanding sport that places significant stress on the body, particularly the hands, fingers, forearms and shoulders. Without adequate rest and recovery time, climbers risk injury and burnout. Rest days are crucial for allowing the body to recover from the strain of climbing. During rest days, climbers should avoid strenuous activity and instead focus on activities that promote relaxation and rejuvenation, such as yoga or stretching.

Climbers who take their recovery time seriously will see improvements in their performance over time. By giving their bodies the time they need to recover between climbs, they will be able to push themselves harder and improve their overall strength and endurance.

Stretching is one of the most critical components of an effective recovery strategy. Stretching helps to release tension in the muscles and reduce soreness, allowing your body to recover more quickly. It also helps to increase flexibility, which can improve overall performance on future climbs. Hydration is another crucial element of post-climbing recovery.

Drinking plenty of water helps to flush out toxins from the body and prevent dehydration, which can lead to muscle cramps and fatigue.

Proper nutrition is also essential for effective recovery after climbing. Eating a balanced diet with plenty of protein can help repair damaged muscles and support overall health.

Finally, rest is perhaps the most crucial component of an effective recovery strategy. One common mistake climbers make in managing their recovery time is not allowing enough time for rest and recovery. Climbing can be a demanding sport, and the body needs time to recover from the physical stresses placed on it. Letting your muscles and tendons recuperate between sessions is as important as sleep.

I took five days rest before free soloing Mickey's Beach Crack 5.12b near Stinson Beach, California, and the same before capturing the first ascent of Maniac 5.13d/14a in Quoddy Head State Park in northeastern Maine. So, the next time you are not feeling strong, you may want to take another rest day. That strategy has always worked for me, and it could work for you.

CLIMBING DISCIPLINES

Chapter 53
CLIMBING DISCIPLINES

"Every form of climbing is a discipline."
Dan Goodwin

We all march to a different drummer. Some prefer bouldering, others, deep water solo or sport. Much will depend on your personality and the level of risk you are willing to take. If you are new to the sport, you may find certain disciplines speak to you, and others, you could take or leave it. That's perfectly normal. There is a discipline for everyone and they all fall under the umbrella of climbing.

BOULDERING: Scaling boulders or short indoor walls.

SPORT CLIMBING: Scaling routes protected with predrilled bolts.

TRAD CLIMBING: Routes protected with climber placed protection.

BIG WALL: Multi pitched routes on rock walls.

PSICOBLOC: Deep Water Soloing (DWS) over the ocean, lake or the deep end of a swimming pool.

FREE SOLO: Free climbing without a rope.

ROPED SOLO: When a climber scales a route alone with a rope, either with aid or free climbed.

SPEED CLIMBING: When a climber scales a route or big wall like the Nose of El Capitan in Yosemite Valley for time. Speed Climbing is also an Olympic sport.

MOUNTAINEERING: Scaling mountains such as Mt. Everest or K2.

ICE CLIMBING: Scaling frozen waterfalls with ice axes and crampons.

DRY TOOL CLIMBING: Scaling iceless cliffs or artificial walls with ice axes and crampons.

AID CLIMBING: Ascending with the aid of trad placements.

BUILDERING: Scaling a building - either free or with the aid of suction cups, skyhooks, or custom-made equipment.

TICK TYPES

Chapter 54
TICK TYPES

"Every variation of climbing is a discipline."
Dan Goodwin

Nothing beats the feeling of sending. The sense of achievement can be profound. However, it's essential to know the various forms of ascent known as Tick Types. To receive credit for a send, you must climb the route cleanly.

That is, you must free-climb a route or boulder problem using nothing but your hands and feet. Under no circumstances can you receive tension from the rope; grab a quickdraw or a bolt anchor.

The same rule applies to bouldering.

You are not allowed to dab your foot on the ground or to receive an assisted spot. If either of these scenarios happens, you should respond honestly.

"I did the route with a few hangs."

Or..."I sent the problem with a dab."

Climbers will respect your honesty. Nobody likes it when someone falsely claims they sent a route or boulder problem. Resist this temptation. The only person you will be short-changing is yourself.

To receive credit for an ascent, you must successfully free climb the entire route until you clip the anchors or reach the top of a boulder problem. Slapping the top doesn't count.

You must pull over the top or clip the anchors for that ascent to count. When bouldering indoors, you must latch the top or last hold with both hands - just as you have seen in the Olympics.

Within this definition of free climbing, there are three categories. The highest level is the **Onsight Ascent**, when a person sends a route on their first shot, sight unseen, without any form of beta, whether verbally or visually, and that includes video viewing.

In the 1980s, many climbers looked the other way while belaying to keep their onsight clean. Admittedly, this was an unsafe practice.

So, as a rule, if you find yourself in this situation and want credit for an onsight, please have someone else belay so you can look the other way. Do not embrace the old school of thinking for purity's sake. There is too much room to make mistakes when so much is at stake.

Always keep safety first.

The second highest level is the **Flash Ascent**.

At the time of this publication, Adam Ondra, the climbing phenomena from the Czech Republic, became the first person to flash a 5.15a/9a+ by sending Supercrackinette (first established by Alex Megos) in the South of France on his first shot.

The difference between Onsight and Flash is vast. With **Onsight**, you cannot receive any form of visual or verbal beta.

While with a **Flash** ascent, you are allowed to have prior knowledge, whether it's watching another climber, viewing videos, inspecting the holds on rappel, or receiving verbal beta.

"Don't use that hold. Bump to the next and cross with your right."

Naturally, within these categories, there are subcategories. Some argue that those who place their gear should have a higher distinction. I could not agree more. Anyone that has carried a rack of draws or trad gear can testify to that. It's a whole different ballgame.

Not only is the climber saddled with the weight, which can throw off your balance and affect your ability to make a difficult move, but the climber doesn't have the luxury of clipping a line of pre-placed draws or trad gear. They are charging into the unknown, placing quickdraws or trad gear as they go.

However, when you fail to send the route on your first shot, you can no longer claim credit for an Onsight or a Flash. From then on, whether you send it on your next attempt or your hundredth, the only credit you can claim is a **Red Point** ascent.

And there is nothing wrong with that. Just because you don't capture an onsite or a flash doesn't mean your ascent isn't worthy. If anything, redpointing a route can be a crown achievement at any grade. Silence 5.15d, La Dura Dura 5.15c, Jumbo Love 5.13b, and even my ascent of Maniac 5.13d are all redpointed first ascents.

If it weren't for redpointing, climbing would not have evolved into today's sport. If anything, redpointing a route is a rock warrior's way of embracing the '*Never Give Up*' attitude.

If you fail on your first shot, take a 30-minute break or longer, depending on your pump, and try again. Some of the most challenging routes in the world, including Dawn Wall in Yosemite Valley, took years to free climb cleanly. And if you embrace this attitude, the same can happen to you

.

CLIMBING GRADES

Chapter 55
BOULDERING GRADES

In the 1970s and 80s, bouldering grades were ruled by the B-system, which was conceived by **John Gill** in the 1950's. The B1 grade was allocated to problems that were more difficult than any roped climb. The B2 grade was for problems harder than any roped routes that hadn't been scaled yet. While the B3 grade was awarded to problems that was only sent once but attempted by many. Once repeated, the grade would automatically be lowered to B2+, making it extremely difficult to distinguish the difference. Hence, the introduction of V-grading system.

In the 1990s, John Sherman a.k.a. Vermin, developed the open ended numeric system while establishing many of the most challenging problems at Hueco Tanks, near El Paso, Texas. I took the liberty of extending the V-grading system to V20 as an enticement for future generations.

If you use the following bouldering grade chart as a guide, and make your route selection accordingly, you will likely pick a route within your ability and increase your odds of sending.

USA	FONT	GBR	BRZ
VB	3		1
V0-	4-	B1	II
V0	4		III
V0+	4+	B2	IV
V1	5		IV sup
V2	5+	B3	V
V3	6A	B4	VI
	6A+		VI
V4	6B	B5	VI sup
	6B+		VI sup
V5	6C	B6	7a
	6C+		7b
V6	7A	B7	7c
V7	7A+	B8	8a
V8	7B	B9	8b
	7B+		8c
V9	7C	B10	9a
V10	7C+	B11	9b
V11	8A	B12	9c
V12	8A+		10a
V13	8B	B13	10b
V14	8B+	B14	10c
V15	8C	B15	11a
V16	8C+	B16	11b
V17	9A	B17	11c
V18	9A+	B18	12a
V19	9B	B19	12b
V20	9B+	B20	12c

Chapter 56
LEAD CLIMBING GRADES

The evolution of lead climbing grades in the United States can be traced back to the 1930s, when climbers began using a system of letters to indicate the difficulty of a climb. This system was later refined in the 1960s by Yvon Chouinard and Royal Robbins, who created the Yosemite Decimal System (YDS). The YDS uses numbers to indicate the difficulty of a climb, with 5.0 being the easiest and 5.15 currently the most difficult. As lead climbing became more popular, additional sub-grades were added to indicate the difficulty of leading a climb, including 'a' 'b", 'c', and 'd'.

When climbing in another country use the comparison chart as a reference. As you will quickly discover, one route may feel easy because it plays to your strengths, while the other routes of the same grade may seem nearly impossible. But one thing is certain, outdoor grades are always stiffer than indoor climbing gyms.

Just because you send 5.12s in the gym doesn't mean you should be able to do the same outdoors. You may disagree with the grade, but don't let this get into your head. An astute climber will use the grades as a gauge. If the route feels easy, you can try something harder, just as you would with weight training.

Use the grades the same way. Not only will this method help you send more consistently, but it can also keep you safe.

YDS	UK	FR	UIAA	AUS	AF	BRZ
5.0				3-4	3-4	I sup
5.1	2	2	II	5-6	5-6	II
5.2				7	7	
5.3	3	3	III	8-9	8-9	III
5.4		4a	IV	10	10	III sup
5.5	4a	4b	IV+/V-	11-12	11-12	IV
5.6	4b	4c	V	13	13	
5.7	4c	5a	V+	14-15	14-15	
5.8		5b	VI-	16	16	IV sup
5.9	5a	5c	VI	17	17-18	V
5.10a		6a	VI+	18	19	VI
5.10b	5b	6a+	VII-	19	20	
5.10c		6b	VII	20	21	VI sup
5.10d	5c	6b+	VII+		22	
5.11a				21		7a
5.11b		6c	VIII-	22	23	7b
5.11c	6a	6c+		23	24	7c
5.11d		7a	VIII-	24	25	
5.12a		7a+	VIII+	25	26	8a
5.12b		7b		26	27	8b
5.12c	6b	7b+	IX-	27	28	8c
5.12d		7c	IX-	28	29	9a
5.13a		7c+	IX+	29	30	9b
5.13b		8a			31	9c
5.13c	6c	8a+	X-	30	32	10a
5.13d		8b	X	31	33	10b
5.14a	7a	8b+	X+	32	34	10c
5.14b		8c		33	35	11a
5.14c	7b	8c+	XI-	34	36	11b
5.14d		9a	XI	35	37	11c
5.15a	8a	9a+	XI+	36	38	12a
5.15b		9b		36	39	12b
5.15c	8b	9b+	XII-	38	40	12c
5.15d		9c	XII	39	41	13
5.16a		9c+	XII+	40	42	13a

CLIMBING GLOSSARY

Abseil: European/Australian word for rappelling

Accessory Cord: Static cords made of Kevlar or Spectra.

ACD (Active Camming Device): Spring-loaded protection device for rock cracks and pockets.

Active Protection: Climbing protection with spring-loaded cams or sliding wedges.

Aid Climbing: The opposite of free climbing with hands and feet, climber relies on protective devices, slings, skyhooks, ropes, or jumars to assist their ascent. Grades of difficulty (A1-A5).

Anchor: A secure anchor (two or more bolts or protection devices) that can secure a belayer, catch a fall, hoist a load, or be used for top roping or rappelling.

ANSI (American National Standards Institute): An agency that enforces industrial standards.

Approach: The trail or hike to the base of a route.

Arete A sharp edge formed by two intersecting rock planes.

Armbar Arm position formed by pressing a palm against one side of a crack with the elbow against the other. Used for climbing squeeze chimneys and off width cracks.

Ascender: a.k.a. Jumars. A mechanical device that enables a climber to ascend a rope when aid climbing or caving, haul heavy bags, and perform lifesaving rescue operations.

ASTM (American Standards for Testing and Materials): An agency that establishes materials specifications and testing standards.

Auto-Lock: A twisting spring-loaded mechanism on a carabiner gate that self closes and locks.

B

Back Clip: The act clipping a rope into a quickdraw from the outside to the inside instead of the other way around. Considered dangerous because the rope can unclip itself.

Back Step: Stepping on a hold with the outer edge of the foot.

Backup: Installing additional climbing protection to backup an anchor.

Barn Door: The swinging motion a climber experiences when off balance.

Bashie: A malleable anchor that is bashed into a small crack or fissure when aid climbing.

Belay: The act of managing the rope or arresting a fall, whether on top rope or lead. Usually requires a belayer or an auto belay system for top ropes.

Belayer: The person that manages the rope, catches a fall, and lowers.

Bent-Gate Carabiner: A bent gate carabiner on the rope-clipping end of a quickdraw.

Beta: Shared information regarding the sequence of moves on a boulder problem or lead route. Beta can be shared verbally or via observation, whether in person or video.

Bight: A folded or bent section of rope.

Big Wall: A multi-pitch rock climb like El Capitan in Yosemite Valley, California

Biomechanics: The study of muscular mechanics.

Bivouac: An overnight encampment on a big wall or ground or without a tent.

Bivy: An abbreviated word for bivouac.

Body Belay: To belay with rope around the belayer's back when a device is not available.

Bolted Route: A sport-climbing route protected with bolt anchors, whether indoors or out.

Bolts: A drilled expansion bolt for protection with hangers to clip ropes.

Bombproof: An anchor or hold that considered unbreakable.

Bottleneck: Route that converges with others or a crack that tapers for trad protection.

Bouldering: Rope-free climbing on boulders of various heights or base of route.

Bowline: Knot that can be attached to a harness or anchors. Not as safe as Figure-8.

Brake hand: The hand used to prevent the rope from sliding through a belay device.

Bucket: A large hold that is easy to grip. Also known as Jug.

C

Camelot: A spring-loaded camming device made by Black Diamond.

Camming: When a spring-loaded device or wire stopper rotates and wedges against two opposing sides of crack.

Camming Device: Climbing protection that wedges into a crack or pocket.

Cambered Sole: The arched sole of a climbing shoe with a down-turned toe.

Carabiner: A lightweight metal oval with a spring gate for clipping a rope.

Caving: Exploring caves with the climbing equipment.

CEN: European Committee that establishes safety requirements for climbing gear.

Chalk: Gymnast chalk (Carbonate of Magnesium) is used for better grip.

Chalk Bag: A drawstring pouch used for chalk. Small pouches are worn when climbing. Larger containers with flat bottoms are reserved for bouldering.

Chest Harness: A chest harness used in combination with a seat harness to maintain an upright position when rappelling or jumaring with a heavy pack.

Chimney: A wide crack large enough for a climber to move upward by using opposing force with their body, hands, and feet.

Chock: Passive protection wedged into a crack with a cord and carabiner for clipping a rope.

Chock Pick: A tool used to extract a passive protection.

Chockstone: A rock wedged in a crack.

Clean: 1. When a route is free of dirt and debris. 2. When the second person climbing removes the protective gear placed by the lead climber. 3. When the lead climber frees the routes without using any gear to aid their ascent.

Climber: The person ascending the rock face or climbing wall.

Climbing: The act of ascending a rock, snow, ice, or climbing wall surface.

Clove hitch: A knot used for tying the climbing rope to an anchor.

Cordage: A static cord used for climbing applications.

Cordelette: A long cord tied to a three-point, equalized anchor system.

Core: The center of a climbing rope.

Crack: A fissure in a rock or artificial climbing wall.

Crag: A term used to describe a climbing area.

Crimper: A small edge wide enough for the fingertips.

Crux: The toughest single move or sequence of moves on a climbing route.

D

Daisy Chain: A runner with multiple loops for creating an adjustable anchor.

Dead Point: When a climber reaches for a hold at the apex of their upward movement.

Dihedral: An open-book formation. Also referred to as a "corner." Opposite of an arete.

Directional: A strategically placed protection device to prevent a climber from swinging on a route that involves a traverse or an overhang.

Drop Knee: The act of dropping the knee to hold the climber's body next to the cliff or wall.

Dyno: When a climber leaps dynamically for a hold or sequence of holds.

Double Runner: A length of webbing used to attach climbing protection to the rope.

Drag: The friction generated as a rope passes through series of clips not following a straight line.

Dry-Treated: Ropes that have been treated with a water-repellent.

Dynamic: 1. Ropes that stretch to absorb the impact of a fall. 2. When a climber lunges for the next hold. See dyno.

E

Edging: When a climber stands on the edge of a climbing shoe.

EN (European Norm): Products that meet CEN standards.

Equalized: An anchor that equally distributes the weight to each piece of protection.

F

Face: A wall of rock or ice on a cliff or mountain - such as the North Face of the Eiger.

Face Climbing: When a person scales a rock face instead of crack climbing.

Fall Factor: 1. The likelihood of a climber falling. 2. A formula that calculates the severity of a fall by dividing the length of a fall by the amount of rope in play.

Finger Crack A crack in a wall the size of a person's fingers.

Figure 4: When a climber hooks a foot on their arm for additional support.

Figure 8: A knot resembling a figure 8 when tying a rope into a climber's harness.

Finger-Lock: When a climber wedges their fingers into a crack.

Fist Jam: When a climber wedges their fist into a crack.

Fixed Protection: Gear permanently anchored to a wall or crack such as a bolt or piton.

Flash: When a person scales a route on the first try after watching another person climb the route in person, via video, or informed verbally.

Fisherman's knot: A knot used for attaching two accessory cords or ropes together.

Flared: A crack that flares outwards instead of inward.

Follow: To ascend a route to collect the protection or quickdraws left by the lead climber.

Free Climb: To scale a rock face or climbing wall with hands and feet only.

Free Rappel: To descend a rope via rappel without contacting the rock.

Free Solo: When a person free climbs a rock, ice, or mountain face without a rope.

Friction: To grip the rock surface with a pair of climbing shoes or hands.

Friends: Invented by Ray Jardin in 1978. See spring-loaded camming devices.

G

Gaston: When a climber pushes in the opposite direction.

Gate: The spring-loaded opening on a carabiner. Gate can be straight, bent, or locking.

Girth Hitch: A knot made with a runner or sling for fixed objects.

Grigri: An auto-locking belay device for belaying and catching a climber's fall.

Gripped: When a climber is paralyzed by fear.

Gym: Indoor climbing facility.

H

Half Rope: A smaller diameter rope (8.2 to 9mm) that is often used in pairs utilizing alternating pieces of protection to minimize the distance a climber falls while clipping.

Hand Crack: A crack that fits an entire hand, but not so wide it requires a fist jam.

Hang Dog: To take tension while lead climbing to rest and assess the moves. Once considered unethical in the 1970s and early 80s.

Hand Jam: The act of jamming a hand into a crack by cupping the palm.

Hanging Belay: Belaying while suspended from anchors on a multi-pitch route when ledges are not available.

Harness: A padded waist belt and leg-loop system for tying into a rope, belaying, or rappelling.

Hexcentric: A 6-sided protection device that wedges into a crack with threaded 5.5mm cord.

Heel Hook: A technique used on overhanging walls, roofs, traverses, and aretes to enable the climber to rest or negotiate a move.

Highball: A taller than average boulder problem with consider risk of injury or death.

Huecco Scale: A grade system for bouldering conceived by John Sherman, a.k.a. "The Verm," while climbing in Huecco, Texas in the late 1980s. Also known as the V-Scale.

I

Interactive Climbing Walls: Also known as SICTBs (standardized interactive climbing training boards.

J

Jam: When a climber wedges a finger, hand, or foot into a crack to ascend or descend a route.

Jug: A large hold that is easy to grip. Also known as Bucket.

Jumar–The original mechanical ascender, often applied to all brands of ascenders. Also the term for using an ascender.

K

Kernmantle–Nylon climbing rope construction consisting of a core (kern) covered by a braided outer sheath (mantle).

Kevlar®–Strong, light fiber made by DuPont used in bulletproof vests. Used in climbing cord for its high tensile strength and resistance to cutting.

Kilonewton (kN): A quantifiable measure of force when falling using Newton's Law.

Kneebar: When a climber wedges a knee beneath a rock feature to gain access or rest.

L

Last: 1. The molded form in the sole of the shoe. 2. The last person to climb.

Lead: The first person to scale a route and place or clip preplaced gear while being belayed.

Leg loops: The leg loops that attach to the waist belt of climbing harness.

Lie Back: To lean one way or the other while ascending a crack or flake.

Lock Off: When a climber locks their arm into a bent position to clip or to grab another hold.

Lower: When a belayer lowers the lead or top rope climber to the ground or belay station.

M

Mantel: The act of pressing downward on a ledge or top of boulder with the palm of hand.

Mono: A pocket large enough for a single finger, often the middle. Also known as Mono Doigt.

Multi-Pitch: A route requiring additional belay stations.

Munter Hitch: A knot tied to a locking carabiner for the purpose of belaying.

N

Nut: A metal wedge of various sizes affixed to a rubber coated cable for clipping carabiners.

Nut Tool: A metal pick used for removing wire nuts stuck in a crack.

O

Off-Width: A crack wider than the fist but not wide enough to be a chimney.

On Sight: When a climber scales a route on their first shot without any prior knowledge of the route or moves. Zero Beta. Considered the highest level in sending.

P

Passive Protection: A protection device used for climbing without any moving parts such as hexcentric chocks or wire stoppers.

PCD (passive camming device): An acronym for a camming device without moving parts such as hexcentric chocks or wire stoppers. Opposite of ACD.

Perlon: A European term for a nylon accessory cord.

Permadraw: A steel cable with a clipping carabiner, attached a fixed bolt and a locking carbineer, eliminating the need to place or retrieve quick draws.

Pitch: The length between belay stations or the top of a route.

Piton: A steel wedge pounded into a crack for aid climbing. Forbidden in most climbing areas due to the scarring.

Placement: The act of inserting climbing protection into a crack.

Protection: A climbing device used to secure a rope to the rock, ice, or mountain face to catch a climber in the event of a fall.

Prusik Knot: Named after Karl Prusik, an Austrian mountaineer in 1931, who used the friction hitch knot to ascend a fixed rope on several summits.

Pumped: When a climber's forearms are about to explode, making it impossible to grip the largest holds or make the next clip.

Q

Quickdraw: A synthetic runner of varying lengths with a carabiner on either end for connecting a rope to a bolt or trad gear placement.

R

Rack: Gear used to climb a route, whether single pitch or multiple.

Rand: The outer strip of rubber on a climbing shoe.

Rappel: A technique used to descend a cliff or mountain face on a rope.

Ratings: A grade of difficulty given to a route.

Red Point: A successful free climb ascent after failing to secure an on-sight or flash.

Redundant: Installing more than one anchor as backup.

Retiring: Disposing climbing gear due to age or damage. Recommended practice.

Route: The path or sequence of moves or clips on a wall, rock, ice, or mountain face.

Runner: A length of webbing used to attach a rope to protection.

Runout: The distance between the last clipped piece of protection and the lead climber.

S

Sandbag: When a climber recommends or grades a route that is considerably more difficult than stated with the hope their partner or others will flail and fail.

Screamer: When a climber screams while taking a fall on lead.

Screw Lock: A locking carabiner gate that screws tight.

Second: The person that climbs the route second, usually after belaying the lead climber.

Semi-Flexed: A climbing shoe that mimics the foot like slippers.

Send: To climb a route without falling or resting on gear.

Sewing-Machine Legs: When a climber's legs shake uncontrollably under stressful situations.

Sheath: The protective covering on a climbing rope or cord.

Shock Load: The force exerted when a weight is dropped onto an anchor or rope.

Side Pull: When a climber grips a vertical edge and leans to the side.

Single rope: A climbing rope certified to catch X number of leader falls.

Single runner: A length of webbing used to extend anchors.

Sloper: A sloping hold that forces a climber to grip with an open hand.

SLCD (Spring-Loaded Camming Device: Invented by Ray Jardin in 1978. See Friends. Today, companies offer sizes ranging from pinky fingers to larger than fist.

Slipper: A flexible climbing shoe that fits like a slipper.

Smear: To press the ball of a climbing shoe against the rock or wall for maximum friction.

Solo: To scale a rock, ice, or mountain face alone with gear - either free or with aid.

Spec: Specifications for a product.

Spectra: A cord that is 10X stronger than steel by weight and 2X as strong as Kevlar.

Speed Climbing: When climbers race up a speed climbing wall or cliff like the Nose of El Capitan in Yosemite Valley, California.

Sport Climbing: 1. A form of rock or indoor wall climbing using pre-placed bolts as protection. 2. Term coined by Dan Goodwin in the early 1980s with the First International Sport Climbing Championship at Snowbird, Utah, and his company Sport Climbing Systems.

SRENE: Acronym for Solid, Redundant, Equalized and No Extension. The desired merits for a climbing anchor.

Static: A non-stretch climbing rope for rescue and caving. Not recommended for leading.

Stemming: When a climbers presses opposing walls in a dihedral, corner or chimney.

Sticht Plate: Invented by Franz Sticht, a German mountaineer in the late 1960s. The devise consists of a steel or aluminum plate with two holes for a doubled rope rappel or belay.

Stick Clip: A telescopic devised used to preplace quickdraws when clipping the first bolt is deemed risky. Widely accepted and encouraged at most sport climb areas.

Stopper: A forged wedge with a coated wire cable or Kevlar for clipping carabiners and ropes.

Stopper Knot: A knot at the rope's end to prevent from sliding through a belay or rappel device.

Swami: A belt made of 2" webbing wrapped around the waist, commonly used as a climbing harness in 1970s. Not considered safe. A swami is also the waist-belt of a climbing harness.

T

TCU (Three-Cam Unit): A spring-loaded camming device that only requires three cams, vs the four-cam device created by Ray Jardin in 1978. Conceived in 1983 by Doug Phillips, the owner of Metolius in Bend, Oregon.

TDR (Thermodynamic Rubber): The synthetic rubber used for climbing shoes.

Three-Point Suspension: 1. When a climber maintains three points of contact with rock.　　2. Three opposing pieces of protection for a belay or rappel station

Thin Hand Crack: A crack that will not accept the entire hand, but not tight enough to be a finger jam. Considered one of the more difficult sizes to climb. Super Crack 5.12c in Gunks.

Toe Displacement: The degree a climbing shoe curves the foot toward the inside edge.

Top Rope: When a rope hangs from a fixed anchor at the top of a climbing wall or cliff.

Traditional or Trad: Climbing with protection that must be placed by the lead climber.

Traverse: To move laterally (sideways) on the rock, ice, mountain, or climbing wall.

Tube Chock: An aluminum tube that wedges into a wide crack for protection.

Twin Rope: Climbing with two strands of rope running through the alternating protection.

U

UIAA: Swiss based organization founded in 1932 to promote and protect mountaineering worldwide, and to ensure the safety of climbing equipment.

Undercling: The underside of a rock flake or climbing hold that requires the climber to grip the edge with the palm up versus palm down.

W

Water Knot: A knot that ties two ends of flat webbing together. Also known as a ring bend.

Webbing: Woven nylon tape used for making slings and runners for climbing.

Wedge: A tapered aluminum wedge with a wire cable or cord for protecting cracks.

Whipper: When the lead climber takes a long fall.

Z

Z-Clipping: A clipping mistake where a climber pulls a length of rope up from below their last-placed placed piece of protection and then clips their next piece of gear.

Zipper–A series of protection placements that pop out in sequence when the leader falls. Often coincides with a screamer.

ABOUT the AUTHOR

Dan Goodwin, a.k.a SpiderDan, is a renowned American climber and the forefather of sport climbing. His daring free solos and flag maneuvers on National TV and historic building ascents made him a household name, especially when he commentated for CBS Sports at the First International Sport Championship in Snowbird, Utah, and free soloed both sides of the CN Tower (world's tallest structure) in Toronto, Canada.

Today, Goodwin continues to climb and inspire others while adding the final touches to his autobiography **Untethered** - When Success is Your Only Option.

If you are interested in receiving information regarding the publication date, workshops, or lectures, please **SIGN UP!**

Made in United States
Troutdale, OR
12/11/2023

15701711R00104